*OIKO*NOMICS

HOW TO INVEST
IN LIFE'S FIVE CAPITALS
THE WAY JESUS DID

MIKE BREEN & BEN STERNKE
with the 3DM TEAM

OIKONOMICS:
How to Invest in Life's Five Capitals
the Way Jesus Did
© Copyright 2014 by Mike Breen and Ben Sternke

First printing 2014
Printed in the United States of America
1 2 3 4 5 6 7 8 9 10 Printing/Year 16 15 14 13 12 11

Cover Design: Blake Berg
Interior Design: Pete Berg

ISBN: 978-0-9852351-7-8

TABLE OF **CONTENTS**

CREDITS

AUTHORS	Mike Breen and Ben Sternke
EDITORS	Robert Neely
	Matt Tebbe
DESIGN	Blake Berg
INTERIOR DESIGN	Pete Berg
PRODUCTION	Libby Culmer

SUPPORT

Beccy Beresic	Phil Beresic	Kimberly Berg
Julie Bird	Tom Blaylock	Sandi Blaylock
Sally Breen	Sam Breen	Taylor Breen
Gavin Culmer	Angela Davila	Anthony Davila
Si Ford	Joan Gooley	Ben Hardman
Sarah Hardman	Jessie Harrelson	Nicole Lee
Eric Pfeiffer	Kandi Pfeiffer	Nik Pfeiffer
Becky Rabb	Jo Rapps	Kevin Rapps
Courtney Reichley	David Reichley	Dave Rhodes
Kim Rhodes	Brandon Schaefer	T.J. Schaefer
Susan Sisson	David Sisson	Deb Sternke
Sharon Tebbe		

CHAPTER 1 | **CAN YOU HAVE IT ALL?**

The annual player draft for the National Football League (NFL) has become an increasingly popular event over the past few years. Young college football players eagerly await the painstakingly researched decisions of the NFL teams that are selecting their next round of recruits to receive lucrative contracts and nearly instant stardom. We watch the proceedings in large part to watch the young men being drafted hit the jackpot. Surely they'll be set for life with the salaries and signing bonuses they are offered. From all appearances, these guys will have it all.

This was certainly the assumption when the Oakland Raiders drafted quarterback JaMarcus Russell as the first overall pick of the 2007 NFL draft. Russell had an outstanding college football career before he signed a contract that guaranteed him $32 million. Russell was eventually released by the Raiders for inconsistent play, but not before he had netted $40 million in salary and bonuses.

We would expect someone like that to be set for life, even without a long NFL career. However, only a few years after leaving the NFL, Russell fell behind on his mortgage payments and had to pay off a lien to the State of California for back taxes he owed. His story of financial ruin isn't an isolated incident. In fact, by the time NFL players have been retired for two years, 78 percent have gone bankrupt or are under financial stress because of joblessness or divorce.

If you found out that 78 percent of the people in your career went bankrupt two years after retiring, you might think about a career switch! Although there are multiple complex reasons for why this happens to professional athletes, it's remarkable we continue to assume that the kind of salary they earn is a ticket to the good life.

This is the same assumption we make about celebrities. We follow their lives in gossip magazines, imagining what it would be like to have the adoration of the masses and more money than we know what to do with. Yet we also see story after story of celebrities who are decidedly unhappy, caught in addictions and relational strife that often ends tragically. Pop singer Whitney Houston's death from a drug overdose is a recent example. She seemed to have a ticket to the good life, and yet we are realizing her life was filled with heartache and crippling addiction.

SHE SEEMED TO HAVE A TICKET TO THE GOOD LIFE, AND YET WE ARE REALIZING HER LIFE WAS FILLED WITH HEARTACHE AND CRIPPLING ADDICTION.

We also tend to assume that winning the lottery is a ticket to the good life. That's what Billie Bob Harrell, Jr. thought when he won the $31 million Texas Lotto jackpot in the summer of 1997. Billie Bob was nearly broke, constantly moving between low-paying jobs, with a wife and three children to support. The first of his $1.24 million annual payouts seemed like the light at the end of the tunnel. Instead, it was the beginning of a year of hell for the 47-year-old Texan.

At first it seemed like a dream: he quit his job at Home Depot,

**"WINNING THE
LOTTERY IS THE
WORST THING
THAT EVER
HAPPENED TO
ME."**

took his family to Hawaii, donated tens of thousands of dollars to his church, bought cars and houses for friends and family, and even donated 480 turkeys to the poor. But his lavish spending attracted unwanted attention, and he had to change his phone number several times after strangers called to demand donations. He also made a bad deal with a company that gives lottery winners lump-sum payments in exchange for their annual checks that left him with far less than what he had won.

When Harrell and his wife Barbara Jean separated less than a year later, it was the straw that broke the camel's back. His son found him dead inside his home from a self-inflicted gunshot wound on May 22, 1999, shortly before he was set to have dinner with his ex-wife. While family members disputed the idea that Harrell could have committed suicide, he clearly wasn't happy with his life; he'd told a financial adviser shortly before his death that "Winning the lottery is the worst thing that ever happened to me."[1]

When we think about NFL players and lottery winners going broke, we know the "right answer" is to say that the good life isn't just about money. But when we examine the way we decide where to live, what vocation to pursue, how to spend our time, what are the criteria we think about when making those decisions? There must be more if we are to have it all.

• • • • • • • • •

[1] http://newsfeed.time.com/2012/11/28/500-million-powerball-jackpot-the-tragic-stories-of-the-lotterys-unluckiest-winners/slide/billie-bob-harrell-jr/

HAVE YOU MET JOHN?

Surely you've seen something like the following scenario play out in real life. John the computer programmer gets an incredible job across the country, making quite a bit more money than he was before. It's an opportunity he can't pass up. It's good for his family's ability to pay bills and move into a bigger house. He'll advance in his career, opening up even more opportunities in the future.

Sure there are sacrifices his family will need to make. They are leaving family and friends they have known for years, and a church community that has meant a lot to them. But it's all for the greater good! With all the money he'll get from his new job, they'll be able to get things they haven't been able to afford until now. John's wife will be able to have her own studio space for her artwork, the kids will each have their own room (with one to spare!). They'll be able to send the kids to a private school that other parents rave about and even set aside money for the kids to go to college.

So he moves his family to take advantage of this remarkable new opportunity. Initially it feels like a dream come true. His family loves the new house and the amenities of the neighborhood they were able to move into, and John enjoys the challenges and fast pace of his new job. But a few years after the move, the family starts noticing some unintended consequences. John doesn't see his family much because of all the extra hours he must put in at work. His wife's artwork is selling well at the farmers markets and craft fairs she attends, but those events are generally on weekends, which means John and his wife see even less of each other.

The stress of his job seeps into his family life, and many evenings he brings his work home

**AGAIN AND
AGAIN, WE SEE
THOSE WHO SEEM
TO BE ON THE
PATH TO HAVING
IT ALL END UP
WITH HARDLY
ANYTHING. WHAT
ARE WE MISSING?**

with him to work on after dinner, or even during dinner. His kids begin to spend most of their time with friends, and so they grow more and more detached from family life. John's wife spends most of her free time with her new friends in the art world, and before John knows it, they haven't been on a date in almost a year. Before he can blink, it's been five years since his opportunity of a lifetime, and John is divorced and living alone, seeing his kids only every other weekend.

What John thought was his passport to the good life ended up being a one-way ticket to nowhere. And while this is a fictional story, many of us have seen similar scenarios play out in real life. What went wrong? How does an opportunity like that turn into the decision that ruined their lives?

These kinds of stories are all around us. Unhappy celebrities grace the pages of every gossip magazine in every grocery store checkout line, and yet the myth persists that these people "have it all." First-round NFL draft pick. Dream job across the country. Fame and fortune as a celebrity. Winning the lottery. Again and again, we see those who seem to be on the path to having it all end up with hardly anything. What are we missing?

Maybe the question itself is the problem. Can we "have it all"? It's actually a very old question. Almost every philosopher in every part of the world in every time has dealt primarily with two questions: 1) How can I be a good person? 2) How can I live the "good life"? These are ways of asking what it means to flourish as a human being. That's what we're all chasing when we ask whether we can really have it all.

This doesn't mean we are greedy. Part of what it means to be human is wondering what it means to live the good life. We pursue happiness, goodness, abundance, and health. When we get sick, we do everything we can to get better. We invest in our physical health. When we move into a new house, we seek to make the living spaces comfortable. We eat food that tastes good. We heat our homes in the winter. We want our children to have enough. We seek meaningful friendships and want a stable and happy home life with our immediate family. After all, nobody makes New Year's resolutions to eat more junk food and feel worse.

It's hard-wired into us to seek the good life. In a sense, then, every one of us is wondering if we can "have it all."

. . . .

EVER FEEL LIKE SOMETHING'S MISSING?

This was the question on the mind of a wealthy young socialite. He was born into money and power, and was being groomed to continue in it. He was living a good life, doing everything expected of him. Everyone praised him for his intelligence, responsibility, and charm. Yet he felt something was missing. Even though he appeared to be living the good life, he knew it wasn't the full picture. But he couldn't put his finger on what the problem was.

At the same time, a new philosopher traveling in the area was taking the world by storm, saying things that no one had ever heard before, doing new things that astonished people from all around. Some people even said he had supernatural powers! People flocked to his events in such droves that there was almost always standing room only, with many people sent away. His teachings felt revolutionary to many. He talked about how to really live the good life, telling people the secrets of what it means to have it all.

So the wealthy young socialite decided to go meet this new philosopher and ask what he needed to do to get the good life. After attending an event in his city, he approached the new philosopher and, somewhat abashed, quietly asked his question. "Hey, you seem to know a thing or two about the good life. Everyone thinks I have it all, but I'm pretty sure I don't have what you're talking about. What do I need to do to get it?"

The new philosopher replied, "Well, it seems like you already know it—do what's expected of you, hold up your responsibilities, and be good to others."

The socialite responded, "That's what I already do. That's what I've always done, in fact. What am I missing?"

The new philosopher replied, "Aha, I get it. You *really* want to know? Here's the first step — give up your old life, give all the money away, and come hang out with me. I'll show you." At that point the philosopher turned his attention to someone else asking a question, and the socialite disappeared from view.

The wealthy young socialite was aghast at the answer. Leave his whole life? Give all the money away? Step out of all the positions of power? He assumed the answer would be something he could just add to the life he already had. But apparently this was a much deeper issue that he had imagined.

He tossed and turned on his bed that night, contemplating the philosopher's proposition. He tried to imagine himself telling his parents, his friends, his brothers and sisters that he was giving all his money away and going to hang out with a new philosopher. He knew what their questions would be. How will you support yourself? Why are you doing this? Isn't it risky? Who is this philosopher anyway? Have you joined a cult? We know you're going through a phase right now, but don't make any rash decisions…

After a tortuous night of very little sleep, he made a cup of coffee and went off to breakfast with a group of friends. Later that day he had some meetings with a few business partners, and then dinner with his parents that night. He never said anything to any of them and never saw the philosopher again. Eventually the conversation with the philosopher faded from memory, but the ache to really live the good life stayed with him his entire life.

. . . .

THE ACHE IN OUR HEARTS

Many of you will recognize that story above as a retelling of an encounter Jesus had with a rich young ruler. The ruler had money, power, and youth, and he was *righteous*, meaning that he held to the expectations of Jewish law. In the eyes of any first-century Jew, this man had it all.

NOBODY IMAGINES HEAVEN AS A COLD, POVERTY-STRICKEN PLACE WHERE EVERYONE IS SICK AND LONELY. ETERNAL LIFE IS THE GOOD LIFE. JESUS OFFERED THE CHANCE TO ACTUALLY HAVE IT ALL.

And yet he came to Jesus asking what more he needed to do to "inherit eternal life." Eternal life doesn't just mean unending life—it means a flourishing life, a wonderful life. Inheriting eternal life means we are living abundantly, flourishing as human beings in every way. This is the destiny we were created for, the destiny toward which God is pulling us. Think of it this way: nobody imagines heaven as a cold, poverty-stricken place where everyone is sick and lonely. Eternal life is the good life.

This is the heart of the ache the rich young ruler felt that drove him to ask Jesus this question. Despite the ruler's riches, power, and good standing with the community, he recognized in Jesus something he didn't have, some kind of abundance he had no access to.

Eventually Jesus gave it to him straight, saying that the way to get what he wanted was to liquidate his riches, give to the poor, and come and follow as a disciple. We often think that Jesus was being overly harsh with the rich young ruler. After all, this didn't seem to be an entrance requirement for anyone else. Does it mean we all need to sell our possessions? Is it wrong to be rich? How much money counts as "rich" we nervously wonder.

But the reality is that Jesus wasn't being harsh with the rich young ruler. He was actually offering him the opportunity of a lifetime. Think about it: The thing the rich young ruler knew he was lacking was the thing Jesus actually offered him—a chance to inherit eternal life. The opportunity to discover the good life the ruler knew he wasn't fully living. Jesus offered the chance to actually have it all.

As we wonder about having it all, we sometimes think the religious answer to that question is NO. You can't have it all, and the sooner you get used to it, the better. As the Man in Black tells Buttercup in that famous line from *The Princess Bride*, "Life is pain, highness. Anyone who says differently is selling something."

But that's not what Jesus teaches.

Jesus' strange and shocking answer to the rich young ruler was not to tell him he shouldn't seek the good life, *not* that he should suck it up and deal with it. Jesus' answer was basically to offer the rich young ruler an internship in which he would learn how to live the good life. It would cost him everything, but Jesus said the young ruler *could* have it all, and that it was appropriate to seek this goal.

The same offer is extended to us, but to accept it, we must recalibrate our idea of what it means to have it all. Typically we define the good life too narrowly and look for it in all the wrong places.

EVERYTHING IS TAKEN CARE OF

Follow us in this for a bit. In the middle of one of his most famous talks, the Sermon on the Mount, Jesus told his disciples that because they are working with him, they had no reason whatsoever to worry about anything. "Do not worry about your life, what you will eat or drink, or your body, what you will wear."[2]

Stop and think about this for a second. It's an astonishing invitation. Jesus is saying, "If you follow me, you can safely stop worrying about these things. People who don't know God at all are the ones who run after these things and worry about them, but your Father in heaven knows you need them, and he will care for you."

And then here's the kicker: "But seek first his kingdom and his righteousness, and all these things will be given to you as well."[3]

Here's another way to say it. **"If you make it your top priority to be involved in what God is doing and have his goodness increasingly fill your life, everything else will be taken care of."**

· · · · · · · · ·

[2] See Matthew 6:19-34 for the whole context.
[3] Matthew 6:33

THE SECRET TO LIVING THE GOOD LIFE, TO HAVING IT ALL, IS SEEKING GOD'S KINGDOM ABOVE EVERYTHING ELSE AND BECOMING AN APPRENTICE OF JESUS.

The way to have it all is to make sure you're aiming past the target, pursuing the most valuable thing. When you do that, the rest of the good things come with it. Then you're living abundantly. You've inherited eternal life.

Isn't that a staggering promise? Think about whether you really believe it's true. Jesus told his disciples that if they leveraged everything to seek the kingdom by following him, *everything else* would be thrown in as well! In other words, the secret to living the good life, to having it all, is seeking God's kingdom above everything else and becoming an apprentice of Jesus.

This is exactly what the disciples had done. Jesus wasn't asking the rich young ruler to do anything different from what his twelve disciples had done. Peter and Andrew as well as James and John left their nets and followed Jesus. This didn't simply mean they left their nets in the garage and came back later for them. The disciples left their only means of supporting themselves. Fishing was their business, their livelihood. Leaving their nets was quitting their job, leaving their career. It was a big deal! Matthew leaving his tax collector's booth was the same thing; he quit his job and forfeited a lucrative career to follow Jesus.

And for what? Why did they do this? What was it that the disciples gave up everything for? What was it the rich young ruler couldn't just add to his life without reorienting it?

This book is meant to answer **for what?** What is worth giving up everything for? What does it actually mean to live the good life, to have it all, according to Jesus?

We often hear the call to discipleship only through the lens of sacrifice (looking at what we are losing). But Jesus rarely spoke this way! When he talked about discipleship, he always spoke through the lens of investment, looking at what we are gaining. **He promised people that what initially looks and feels like a sacrifice will pay off in the end, which is essentially the same thing as making a good investment.**

Think about these statements from Jesus through the lens of investment.

> *"Whoever finds their life will lose it, and whoever loses their life for my sake will find it."* (Matthew 10:39)

> *"The kingdom of heaven is like treasure hidden in a field. When a man found it, he hid it again, and then in his joy went and sold all he had and bought that field."* (Matthew 13:44)

> *"And everyone who has left houses or brothers or sisters or father or mother or wife or children or fields for my sake will receive a hundred times as much and will inherit eternal life."* (Matthew 19:29)

What's striking about these and other passages is the promise of a return on the investment. It's not just a call to lose your life because it's the right thing to do or because it's what God wants. It's a promise that you'll actually **find real life** if you will only let go of the old one. It's the deal of a lifetime! A free upgrade! A very good investment!

Jesus isn't talking about making a sacrifice because it's the right thing to do. **He's talking about a sacrifice that actually becomes an *investment* that yields a return!**

The man in Jesus' parable who sold all his possessions to buy a field did so *with joy*

"HE IS NO FOOL WHO GIVES WHAT HE CANNOT KEEP TO GAIN WHAT HE CANNOT LOSE." because he found a treasure that was worth a lot more than the sum total of his possessions. He bought the field because it was a great deal, a bargain he couldn't pass up. The promise that there's a treasure in the field you're buying far outweighs the sacrifice you must make to get it.

Jesus encourages us to think about life with God (the kingdom of God) this way. He encourages us to do a cost/benefit analysis on the kingdom and make a wise decision. He encourages us to think pragmatically and economically about it. So that we can do this, he encourages us to think more deeply and broadly about what is actually valuable and worth having.

Seen in this light, the kind of sacrifice Jesus calls us to does not leave us with nothing. It's a sacrifice that becomes an investment, like planting crops that eventually yield a hundredfold return. Jesus calls us to invest—to sell everything and buy the kingdom—because it's actually worth far more than what we currently have. As martyred missionary Jim Elliot said, "He is no fool who gives what he cannot keep to gain what he cannot lose."[4]

This is the integrating principle of an investment strategy that will actually yield what we could call the good life.

So it turns out that seeking the good life is actually what Jesus was all about. In our efforts to have it all we are looking for the right thing. **We're just looking for it in the wrong places.**

· · · · · · · · ·

[4] From a journal entry dated October 28, 1949. Quoted in *The Shadow of the Almighty*, by Elisabeth Elliot.

We believe the quality of your life tomorrow depends on the quantity of your investment today. How can we learn to invest in the right things? Read on as we look to Jesus to answer this question for us.

. . . .

Reflection Questions:

1. Think about what you think heaven will be like. Describe it in as much detail as you can.

2. What kinds of things have you typically invested in to get the good life? Kids' activities? Job promotions? Living near family?

3. Does it surprise you that God actually wants you to flourish as a human being? If so, why?

CHAPTER 2 | **JESUS THE PROSPERITY THEOLOGIAN**

At this point, you might be slightly nervous about what we'll be saying in this book. Are we saying that we ought to *use* Jesus for our personal gain? Are we simply talking about "marrying him for his money"? Is this somehow tied into "prosperity theology" where I rub my Bible three times and a new car appears in the driveway?

Let's not back away from these questions too quickly. If Jesus is really asking us to make investments and expect a return on those investments, we need to explore what kind of return he is talking about. What can we expect will happen when we sell everything to buy the field? What is the buried treasure? If the person who seeks first the kingdom also gets "all these things," what are these things, and what does it look like to seek first the kingdom? If the person who takes Jesus gets everything, what does "everything" mean?

We must ask these questions, even in the extreme, so we can discover what Jesus truly means. We must also make sure we approach these questions from the right perspective.

When we think of "all these things" and "everything," our minds usually go automatically to material wealth. That's how our culture trains us to think, anyway. "Wealth" for us typically refers to financial assets and worldly possessions. So when we hear Jesus talk about a treasure in the field, a return on our investment, we tend to think of *financial* return. But a moment's reflection shows us that a well-lived life (we could call it true wealth) is about much more than finances.

For example, if you become a millionaire but lose all your friends and family, are you wealthy? Is that a good trade-off? Is that a well-lived life? Is it worth losing friends to get more money? If you make more money than everyone else in the world but live in a house by yourself all day with an incurable illness that gives you chronic pain, are you wealthy? Is that a good life? How much money is chronic pain worth? Ask children if they would rather have a rich teacher or a wise teacher? A rich Girl Scout leader or a kind one?

We think most of us would agree a life isn't good if it's filled with financial prosperity but no other kind of flourishing.

Our problem, then, is that our measurement of wealth is too small. It's not that we shouldn't look for a return on our investments—it's that we need to expand our definition of what kind of return we're looking for. We need a new way of evaluating and measuring what actually happens when we make these kinds of investments. We need to think *bigger* about prosperity and wealth.

Our word wealth comes from an old Middle English word that means simply "well-being." God created a perfect world where everything and everyone enjoyed well-being, and although this world has been marred by sin, he is working to restore his world to a state of well-being. That work is what the Bible calls "salvation," which means we can say that God's work of salvation has a lot to do

A WELL-LIVED LIFE IS ABOUT MUCH MORE THAN FINANCES.

JESUS IS THE	:	with wealth! We can call salvation "true wealth." We receive this
TRUE PROSPERITY	:	kind of life by grace and then should invest in order to make it
THEOLOGIAN.	:	grow.

Seen in this light, we could say that Jesus is the true prosperity theologian who is saving us and empowering us to prosper in every way. Our problem is that we still seem to be able to measure only *one way* of prospering.[5] This book is about measuring the other kinds of return on investment we can look for when we invest our lives in the way of Jesus.

. . . .

FROM ECONOMICS TO OIKONOMICS

So, to answer the questions we posed earlier, this is really a book about investment, a book about economics, a book about capital.

But we won't be sharing strategies for making financial investments in mutual funds or stocks. We won't be sharing opinions about advantageous financial policies for governments. No, we want to talk about economics, capital, and investment on a more fundamental, normal, everyday level—the economics of the household, **the everyday life of a family on mission.**

So this is not a book filled with grand, abstract academic theories on economics. It's more like the "home economics" classes you take in school. The kind of economics we're talking about are the normal, everyday things that regular people do every day, such as cleaning

. . . .

[5] Lest you think we have no qualms about prosperity theology, we will talk in chapter 4 about the problems with it.

their houses, taking out the trash, cooking dinner, traveling for work, giving the kids a bath, staying up late at night doing their homework or playing games or reading books, taking a vacation, going out on weekends with their friends, or staying in to watch movies. These normal things are examples of the "home" kind of economics we will be discussing.

This emphasis on home economics is why we named the book *Oikonomics*. The word "economy" comes from the Greek roots *oikos* ("household") and *nomos* ("custom" or "law"), so the original meaning of the word "economy" was "the rule or management of a household." In the ancient world, *oikos* didn't necessarily refer to the physical structures that people lived in, but the network of relationships that constituted the "household," including parents and children, aunts and uncles, sisters and brothers, servants, business partners, and others who functioned together with a common purpose.

We've adopted the word *oikos* to describe the reality of living out our discipleship to Jesus together as a family on mission. Now we take the next step. *Oikonomics* is about how we manage our lives, how we invest our capital as a family on mission to follow Jesus and see his kingdom break in and transform people's lives. It's about the economy of our *oikos*. It's how we do everyday discipleship.

In this book, we're going to move from knowing only how to measure economics (how much money do we have?) to knowing how to measure *oikonomics* (how much true wealth do we have as a family on mission?).

OIKONOMICS IS ABOUT THE ECONOMY OF OUR OIKOS. IT'S HOW WE DO EVERYDAY DISCIPLESHIP.

We begin with the reality that true wealth is **not just about money**. It's about other kinds of capital that we need to identify and learn how to grow. And true wealth is **not just about**

JESUS WAS THE MOST BRILLIANT ECONOMIST WHO EVER LIVED.

me—it's about my whole community flourishing. It's about the common good, not just my individual prosperity.

The person who teaches us how to do *oikonomics* is Jesus. In fact, this book contends that **Jesus was the most brilliant economist who ever lived.**

Admittedly, this hypothesis is somewhat unconventional. We don't usually think of Jesus as an intelligent economist or shrewd businessman who knew how to make an investment. Our culture trains us to think of him as holy, kind, and gracious. But if we're going to follow him as his disciples, we also need to recognize that he was really smart about things that matter. He is an amazing investment strategist. He knows how to make life work well, he knows how to manage a household, he knows how to invest for a return, and most of all he knows how to really *live*. He is the master of the good life.

We won't follow Jesus unless we take him seriously as an insightful person. That's what it means to be his disciple—recognizing that he has the best information about life and putting his teaching into practice.

Why? Because, as Dallas Willard has said, "Jesus isn't just nice, he's brilliant."

So what does it mean to say that Jesus was an economist?

Economists tend to look at the world in terms of **capital**. Capital refers to the goods or assets we have in our possession that we can invest. Economies are built on the exchange of capital. We normally think of capital in terms of monetary value, but there are all kinds of other capitals that economists identify and theorize about. They include land (natural

OUR DEFAULT POSTURE SHOULD BE TO ALWAYS DO THINGS THE WAY JESUS DID THEM.

capital), labor (human capital), knowledge (intellectual capital), infrastructure (public capital), and even brand value (social capital).

All these things and more can be considered forms of capital. The world essentially works as a network of relationships in which we invest particular kinds of capital in particular ways. There are all kinds of ways to slice and dice and recombine and rename these capitals, but Jesus seemed to have a specific way of looking at capital and the realities of economics. As usual, though, he takes us beyond our normal ways of thinking and teaches us how life and capital work in the bigger picture of life with God (or, as the Bible calls it, "the kingdom of God").

Because Jesus takes us beyond simply thinking about one form of capital (money) into all the different forms of capital we have to invest, we call him the true economist. Since he knows how life works, we could call him the great *oikonomist*!

Is it actually important for disciples of Jesus to pay attention to the way Jesus did economics? Yes! Here's why: we firmly believe that the *way* Jesus did things is important. We live by his *words*, we imitate his *works*, but as his disciples we also emulate his *way* of doing things. Our default posture should be to always do things the way Jesus did them. As disciples of Jesus, one of the first questions we ask when we encounter a situation is, "How did Jesus do it?" We could call it **WDJD: What Did Jesus Do?**

WORD

WORKS   WAY

Warren Buffett once said, "Never invest in a business you can't understand." So let's spend some time coming to understand this "kingdom business" that Jesus talks about. How did Jesus practice economics? What was his investment strategy? What is Jesus' way when it comes to stewarding, investing, growing, and multiplying the capital he has for the benefit of others?

That's the way to true wealth. It's the way Jesus our prosperity theologian leads us.

. . . .
Reflection Questions:

1. **Have you ever thought about Jesus as a really smart economist with great investment advice? What surprises you most about this idea?**

2. **Do you really believe that if you seek first the kingdom, which means making it your top priority to be involved in what God is doing, everything else will be taken care of? Have you tried it?**

3. **When you think about Jesus wanting to bring well-being to you and your family on mission, do any fears or concerns rise in your heart? Acknowledge them out loud.**

CHAPTER 3 | **THE ECONOMICS OF JESUS**

Let's talk about heroes and villains. In the recent movie *Man of Steel*, the hero and the villain are very easy to identify. Superman is the hero, sent to Earth to save humanity and urge it toward greatness. General Zod is the villain, seeking to destroy the world for his own gain. Superman confronts Zod in a battle that destroys half of New York, and in the end (spoiler alert!) the hero prevails.

Stories like *Man of Steel* make the heroes and villains easy to spot. Slow, brooding music in a minor key plays over the scene where the villain is revealed, while a bright, energetic, triumphant soundtrack accompanies the hero's scenes. The villains are very clearly motivated by greed or a lust for power, and the heroes are animated by a more selfless motivation.

However, some stories feature unlikely heroes (and unlikely villains). *Lord of the Rings* is a story about the most unlikely of heroes, a hobbit named Frodo. Hobbits are unlikely heroes because they're little, unambitious, and comfort-loving. Yet Frodo is called on a quest for the greater good of Middle Earth. He is an unlikely hero, but a hero nonetheless.

Jesus told a lot of stories, and many of his stories featured unlikely heroes and villains.

ONE OF THE MOST INTERESTING AND DISTURBING FEATURES OF THE VILLAINS OF JESUS' STORIES IS HOW NORMAL THEY ARE.

The story of the Good Samaritan is one. In fact, in Jesus' day the term "Good Samaritan" would have been a laughable oxymoron! Everyone "knew" Samaritans weren't good, which makes Jesus' story all the more explosive.

Here's how it goes. A man is robbed and beaten to within an inch of his life along a dangerous road. A priest who happens to be walking along the same road sees the man lying there, but passes by on the other side of the road. A worker in the temple comes across the man and does the same thing. Finally a good-for-nothing Samaritan sees the man and becomes the unlikely hero of the story by bandaging the man's wounds, carrying him to an inn, and paying for his recovery. The priest and the Levite, whom everyone expected to be the heroes, turned out to be the villains, while the one listeners assumed was a villain turned out to be a hero. Jesus did this a lot in his stories, and it made a lot of people quite angry with him.

One of the most interesting and disturbing features of the villains of Jesus' stories is how *normal* they are. Finding out villains are actually very ordinary people makes us deeply uncomfortable. A historical example of this phenomenon took place in the years after the fall of the Nazi regime in Germany. Adolf Eichmann, one of Hitler's top officials, oversaw the brutal torture and death of countless Jews. Political theorist Hannah Arendt witnessed and reported on Eichmann's trial, during which she was struck by what she called the "banality of evil."[6] She was struck by how Eichmann was a normal person who was just "doing his job." He wasn't particularly anti-Semitic or mentally ill in any way. He was a

· · · · · · · · ·

[6] Banality means something that is boring or ordinary.

very ordinary person following orders and obeying the law. Yet he is one of the worst real-life villains of the twentieth century.

Jesus' villains are disturbingly ordinary as well. In Matthew 25:14-30, Jesus tells a parable about kingdom economics (*oikonomics*). As you read it, pay attention to the investment strategy of the master, and to the person who turns out to be the villain of the story.

> *Again, it will be like a man going on a journey, who called his servants and entrusted his wealth to them. To one he gave five bags of gold, to another two bags, and to another one bag, each according to his ability. Then he went on his journey. The man who had received five bags of gold went at once and put his money to work and gained five bags more. So also the one with two bags of gold gained two more. But the man who had received one bag went off, dug a hole in the ground, and hid his master's money.*

> *After a long time, the master of those servants returned and settled accounts with them. The man who had received five bags of gold brought the other five. "Master," he said, "you entrusted me with five bags of gold. See, I have gained five more."*

> *His master replied, "Well done, good and faithful servant! You have been faithful with a few things; I will put you in charge of many things. Come and share your master's happiness!"*

> *The man with two bags of gold also came. "Master," he said, "you entrusted me with two bags of gold; see, I have gained two more."*

> *His master replied, "Well done, good and faithful servant! You have been faithful with a few things; I will put you in charge of many things. Come and share your master's happiness!"*

Then the man who had received one bag of gold came. "Master," he said, "I knew that you are a hard man, harvesting where you have not sown and gathering where you have not scattered seed. So I was afraid and went out and hid your gold in the ground. See, here is what belongs to you."

His master replied, "You wicked, lazy servant! So you knew that I harvest where I have not sown and gather where I have not scattered seed? Well then, you should have put my money on deposit with the bankers, so that when I returned I would have received it back with interest.

"So take the bag of gold from him and give it to the one who has ten bags. For whoever has will be given more, and they will have an abundance. Whoever does not have, even what they have will be taken from them. And throw that worthless servant outside, into the darkness, where there will be weeping and gnashing of teeth."

Jesus does something in this parable that he does frequently—he uses an economic image to talk about the kingdom of God. To put this in context, biblical scholars tell us the New Testament talks about money approximately *ten times more* than it does about faith. Of course, often when the New Testament talks about money, it's not just about money. It's not giving us financial advice, per se—it's revealing a frame of reference that helps us understand our life. Money is used as a metaphor that helps us understand how life works.

In this parable, Jesus uses a story of financial investment to describe a strategy that he conducts in a person's life as he represents the Father.

Here's his investment strategy: he gives some of his resources to his servants in various amounts and then goes away, expecting that when he returns his servants will have

FOR JESUS, LOSING EVERYTHING ON A BAD INVESTMENT WOULD HAVE BEEN BETTER THAN DOING NOTHING. invested the money and gotten a return on their investment. One servant receives five bags of gold, another two bags of gold, and a third gets one bag of gold.

It's a fairly simple picture. The master entrusts his capital to his servants and expects a return on his investment. The two servants who invested the capital were commended and given more responsibility and privilege within the *oikos*. The third servant, who got one bag of gold, simply didn't invest the money. He was afraid so he just hid it in the ground and gave it back to his master. This servant got something quite different!

From our vantage point, what the master says seems astonishingly harsh: "You wicked, lazy servant!" He gives the poor servant a severe tongue-lashing, takes his money away, and throws him out into the darkness outside the house, "where there will be weeping and gnashing of teeth."

Honestly, we look at that poor guy and think, "He doesn't seem so bad! All he did was nothing." But as we've said, Jesus' villains are very normal, and this disturbs us because we begin to see ourselves in the story. We think doing nothing would be better than trying to invest and losing everything, but for Jesus, losing everything on a bad investment would have been better than doing nothing. For Jesus, **not investing makes you a villain.**

This servant wasn't *trying* to be a villain, but he ended up a villain because, out of a lack of trust in his master and a scarcity mentality, he refused to invest the money. He assumed that failure in investment would be met with punishment, and thus remained passive. He was afraid and remains passive, trying to play it safe. He is an unlikely, accidental villain, but a villain nonetheless, because he doesn't cooperate with the master's investment plan.

It's easy to become an accidental villain. Think about the civil rights movement. A few obvious "villains" were overtly opposed to equal rights for African Americans. But many more *accidental* villains simply did nothing, keeping their heads down, trying not to make waves, never taking the risk of making the heroic journey of becoming liberators.

Or think about the recent housing bubble and worldwide financial crisis. A few intentional villains knew they were gaming the system and making money at other people's expense. But most people were accidental villains who got caught up in the hype trying to make money off an exotic new financial product, inadvertently contributing to a system that caused many people to lose their homes and life savings.

Some people are villains because they intentionally invest in bad things for selfish reasons. Other people end up as villains because they don't invest in the right things, like the third servant in Jesus' parable.

Jesus' stories teach us that heroes *intentionally invest* in the right things. Jesus always vilifies the middle ground of playing it safe. The hero for Jesus is the person who leverages everything on behalf of what really matters. This is another way of saying "seek first the kingdom of God." Jesus' promise to those who do this is that "all these things will be given to you as well." Jesus, the most brilliant economist in the world, promises that those who invest in the right things **will see a return on their investment**, and that return will benefit God, others, and us. It's a win/win/win scenario. This is an astonishing investment guarantee from the Son of God himself!

THE HERO FOR JESUS IS THE PERSON WHO LEVERAGES EVERYTHING ON BEHALF OF WHAT REALLY MATTERS.

The bottom line of this parable is that God is seeking to bless the whole world, and the way he does this is by investing his capital in his people and looking for a return on that investment. God literally invests his capital in us, and he expects a return. The accidental villain is the person who does nothing with the capital God has invested. The hero is the person who invests the capital, trusting Jesus that it will grow.

. . . .

FIVE KINDS OF CAPITAL

If we know that a well-lived life is about more than money, and that God has invested in us for the blessing of ourselves and others, we need to learn to invest in the right things. To do this, we must ask key questions: What kinds of capital has God invested in us, and where can we begin to look for a return?

Another parable of Jesus will shed light on the kind of capital he is talking about.

Pastors from liturgical traditions often call this passage of Scripture "The Vacation Passage," because

1. It often comes up in the lectionary in August, and
2. They always get someone *else* to preach on it!

This strange parable seems to send all the wrong messages and makes for mostly awkward sermon material. No one wants to preach on it because most people think it just doesn't sound like something Jesus would say.

But we actually think what we find in Luke 16:1-13 *is* something Jesus would say (and did say, of course). Let's take a look.

Jesus told his disciples: "There was a rich man whose manager was accused of wasting his possessions. So he called him in and asked him, 'What is this I hear about you? Give an account of your management, because you cannot be manager any longer.'

"The manager said to himself, 'What shall I do now? My master is taking away my job. I'm not strong enough to dig, and I'm ashamed to beg—I know what I'll do so that when I lose my job here, people will welcome me into their houses.'

"So he called in each one of his master's debtors. He asked the first, 'How much do you owe my master?'

"'Nine hundred gallons of olive oil,' he replied.

"The manager told him, 'Take your bill, sit down quickly, and make it four hundred and fifty.'

"Then he asked the second, 'And how much do you owe?'

"'A thousand bushels of wheat,' he replied.

"He told him, 'Take your bill and make it eight hundred.'

"The master commended the dishonest manager because he had acted shrewdly. For the people of this world are more shrewd in dealing with their own kind than are the people of the light. I tell you, use worldly wealth to gain friends for yourselves, so that when it is gone, you will be welcomed into eternal dwellings.

"Whoever can be trusted with very little can also be trusted with much, and whoever is dishonest with very little will also be dishonest with much. So if you have not been trustworthy in handling worldly wealth, who will trust you with true riches? And if you have not been trustworthy with someone else's property, who will give you property of your own?

"No one can serve two masters. Either you will hate the one and love the other, or you will be devoted to the one and despise the other. You cannot serve both God and money."

Reading that parable reminds us why nobody wants to preach on it! That last part about not serving God and money is okay, but what's with the sneaky behavior of the dishonest manager being *commended* by the master? Talk about unlikely heroes and villains. What in the world is Jesus talking about here?

The best way to tackle this parable is to go backward from the ending. In the very last sentence, Jesus seems to distill the parable into a pithy statement that sums up its main message. (Nowadays he could have tweeted it!) When Jesus says, "You cannot serve both God and money," he is saying that we can have only one ultimate point of reference. Eventually, the thing we value highest will win out, whether that is God or money.

He was telling his hearers that their method of assigning value to the elements of the world around them was way off. In fact, this entire parable is about *how to value various forms of capital in order to invest it wisely*.

The first two forms of capital we've identified are **financial capital** (money) and what we might call **spiritual capital** (God, or, more specifically, a relationship with God as a disciple of Jesus). Over and over, in this parable and in all his other teaching, Jesus shows

SPIRITUAL CAPITAL IS DIFFERENT FROM FINANCIAL CAPITAL, AND FAR MORE VALUABLE AND IMPORTANT THAN FINANCIAL CAPITAL.

us that **spiritual capital is different from financial capital, and far more valuable and important than financial capital**.[7] He has to make this point over and over because the world around him had it exactly the wrong way around. Like us, they tended to value financial capital above spiritual capital. They also *equated* financial capital with spiritual capital; the general assumption of the day was that if you were rich it was a sure sign of God's favor on your life. This perspective caused them to make bad investments (by choosing money above God, for example).

We can quickly identify these forms of capital, spiritual and financial, in this parable. But there are other forms of capital in this parable and the rest of the Scripture. What are they? How valuable are they? And how can we learn from Jesus how to invest them for a return?

When the manager realizes he is going to be fired, he begins to think about what to do next. During his thought process he says, "I'm not strong enough to dig." Here he is contemplating one possible way of gaining financial capital after he loses his job: manual labor. We can call this **physical capital**, the amount of time and energy we have available to invest. The shrewd manager realized that he had very little of this capital to invest ("I'm not strong enough to dig") and thus decided it wasn't a great option for him.

That makes three capitals we've identified: **financial** (the most tangible and highly valued by people), **spiritual** (actually the most valuable), and **physical** (apparently somewhere in the middle). What else is there?

· · · · · · · · ·

[7] Case in point: the rich young ruler we discussed earlier.

After contemplating his situation for a bit, the manager says, "I know what I'll do." He comes up with a brilliant idea, one for which he is later praised by his master (which is why this is the parable of the *shrewd* manager). The manager's shrewdness is actually another form of capital—**intellectual capital**. Intellectual capital refers to the ideas, knowledge, and creativity we have to invest. The manager used his capacity to think creatively (his intellectual capital) to come up with an idea for how to survive after he lost his job.

We see the final capital in this passage in the content of the idea the manager comes up with. He uses the last few hours of his authority over his master's financial capital to reduce the debt that several people owed his master. The manager reasoned that this would allow him to be welcomed into their homes after he lost his job. In reducing their debt, he was gaining what we might call **relational capital** with them! He leveraged his **intellectual capital** to come up with the idea of investing **financial capital** in order to grow **relational capital**.

The master recognizes the wisdom in this move (even though the manager was scheming with *his* money) because the manager invests financial, intellectual, and physical capital to gain relational capital. Jesus says this is a great investment. Jesus says it quite bluntly: "Use worldly wealth to gain friends for yourselves."

Many of us wrestle with this verse. Was Jesus really counseling us to buy friends? In fact, we think he was! Jesus is saying it is worth investing your financial capital to grow your relational capital, because relational capital is worth far more than financial capital. That's the punch line of the parable! Jesus tells us to use our money to invest in people's lives so that we get friendship out of it. In other words, recognize the relative value of each kind of capital and make a good investment.

Jesus mentions at least five different forms of capital in this parable (**spiritual, financial, physical, intellectual,** and **relational**), and his point seems to be that part of following him and learning to live in the kingdom of God means valuing various forms of capital correctly and then making good investment decisions based on those values.

. . . .

PEARL-GATE

We see this trajectory throughout the entire Bible, of people who made investment based on gaining certain kinds of capital, whether wisely or poorly.

- Adam and Eve gave away their relational capital with God for intellectual capital — "knowing good and evil."

- Abraham left his family (relational capital) to obey God, going to the new land God had called him to (spiritual capital), letting Lot take the better land (financial capital), and being rewarded for it.

- Peter left his nets (the financial capital of his livelihood) to follow Jesus (spiritual capital). Matthew did the same with his livelihood of tax collecting.

- King Saul was chosen because of an abundance of physical capital (he was tall and handsome), while King David, his successor, had an abundance of spiritual capital. Saul ended his kingly career in ruin, while David is considered Israel's greatest king.

Remember the story of the rich young ruler? He had kept the commandments as well as anyone and had plenty of financial wealth (which was seen in his day as a sure sign of God's blessing and favor). But he knew something was still missing in his life. "What do I still lack?" he asked. You can hear the desperation in his voice.

Jesus' answer is shocking to our ears. "If you want to be complete, go, sell your possessions and give to the poor, and you will have treasure in heaven. Then come, follow me." The young man goes away sad, because he is unwilling to part with his financial wealth and follow Jesus.

But, as we've seen, the real problem with the rich young ruler wasn't that he had wealth—it was that the way he valued his capital was all wrong. He thought his financial capital was worth more than the opportunity to follow Jesus, *but it wasn't*. Jesus was telling the young man that he was trying to obtain the kingdom of God as a product. He didn't understand the true value of a relationship with Jesus. The fact was, this young man was being offered the internship opportunity of a lifetime!

Come and follow me, Jesus says. Something of infinite worth is being offered to you (an abundance of spiritual capital), and all you need to invest to get it is all of your financial capital. It's the bargain of a lifetime, but the rich young ruler didn't see it, because he valued financial capital more highly than spiritual capital. It caused him to make the disastrous decision to walk away from Jesus.

IT'S THE BARGAIN OF A LIFETIME, BUT THE RICH YOUNG RULER DIDN'T SEE IT.

Think about another economic metaphor Jesus used. He said that a relationship with him, and with the Father through him, is like finding a pearl of "great price," which far exceeded the value of anything else. It's like finding a treasure in a field. If you find a treasure of great worth in a field, the smart thing to do is liquidate everything so you can buy the field. That's Jesus' message to us about the value of spiritual capital—it's far more valuable than your money, so you will do well to sell everything to get it. Cash it all in for that one thing that is most valuable. It just makes good economic sense!

That is, if you trust that spiritual capital *really is more valuable* than financial capital.

The rich young ruler didn't take Jesus' investment advice because he valued financial capital more highly than spiritual capital. Jesus' offer didn't seem like a good deal because he was bringing his own value system into the equation. If we're honest, we admit we probably tend to look at things the same way. So Jesus' word comes to us also: *spiritual capital is worth far more than financial capital.* Treat it as such if you want to experience authentic abundant life. The New Testament talks about our faith being of far greater worth than gold (1 Peter 1:7). So investing our "gold" to grow our faith should be an easy decision for us.

Of course this doesn't mean that we are careless with our financial capital. In fact, Jesus seems to indicate that our ability to invest financial capital wisely is a good indication of whether we can be trusted with spiritual capital. "So if you have not been trustworthy in handling worldly wealth, who will trust you with true riches?" When Jesus says "You cannot serve both God and Money," he isn't saying you can only have one or the other, he is saying we can only have one most important capital in our lives. Serving money means that financial capital is most important. Serving God means spiritual capital is most important, which allows our money to serve God.

How do these things work on a practical level? How do we take the economic genius of Jesus and use it to make wise and practical investment decisions in our everyday lives?

That's what the next chapter is all about.

. . . .

Reflection Questions:

1. Do you think of the capital you have as an investment God has made in you or as your own stuff?

2. Do you value capital in the same way Jesus does? Where are there differences?

3. Have you ever made a decision to choose some other form of capital above spiritual capital? What were the results?

CHAPTER 4 | **THE FIVE CAPITALS OUTLINED**

What we see in Jesus' parable, the rest of the Scriptures, and our experience of life itself is that there are at least five different forms of capital at play in our lives. Five different forms of resource that we possess and are able to invest. Five different capitals that we are in charge of stewarding for God's kingdom as disciples of Jesus.

We've talked about these five capitals in narrative form, and now we're going to get practical. The first thing to realize is that there are five capitals (not just one or two), and the second thing to realize is that it's vital to make sure we understand the relative value of these capitals so we can make wise decisions. The five capitals only work together when they are valued rightly.

On the next page there is a list of the five forms of capital, listed in order of value— spiritual capital is at the top because it is the most valuable, financial capital is at the bottom because it is the least valuable. (We'll talk about why each capital is listed where it is in the value order a bit later.)

1.  SPIRITUAL CAPITAL

How much **spiritual equity** do we have to invest?
The currency is wisdom and power.

2. RELATIONAL CAPITAL

How much **relational equity** do we have to invest?
The currency is family and friends.

3. PHYSICAL CAPITAL

How much **time and energy** do we have to invest?
The currency is hours and health.

4. INTELLECTUAL CAPITAL

How much **creativity and knowledge** do we have to invest?
The currency is concepts and ideas.

5. FINANCIAL CAPITAL

How much **treasure** do we have to invest?
The currency is money: dollars and cents, pounds and pennies, etc.

Let's look at each capital in more depth to see what it is, how it functions, what its currency is, how to invest it, and how to grow it. We'll start with least valuable (financial) and end with the most valuable (spiritual).

FINANCIAL CAPITAL

FINANCIAL CAPITAL IS HOW MUCH **TREASURE** WE HAVE TO INVEST. THE CURRENCY OF FINANCIAL CAPITAL IS, OF COURSE, MONEY: **DOLLARS AND CENTS**, POUNDS AND PENNIES, ETC.

Lowest in our hierarchy is **financial capital**. We are most familiar with this one, because we work with it every day. Financial capital is simply the money we have available to invest. Although this is easy to understand conceptually, we can easily get into trouble in the way that we relate to it and thus invest our financial capital. This typically happens in one of two ways:

The first way we get into trouble is by **overvaluing financial capital**. Society in our today (just as in Jesus' day) often values financial capital as the most important thing in life. We sacrifice all kinds of other capital to get it, even though it never quite fulfills its promises to us. Countless stories, books, and movies share the storyline of risking everything for the big financial payoff.

In fact, studies have shown that, after a certain threshold of income is reached, obtaining more money has almost no effect on our overall happiness or quality of life.[8] As soon as we have enough, getting more money doesn't really seem to create more satisfaction with life. Yet we continue to behave as if it will!

We need to listen to what Jesus tells about the relative value of financial capital; that it is

• • • • • • • • •

[8] One such study from 2010 can be found at
http://content.time.com/time/magazine/article/0,9171,2019628,00.html.

BEING POOR DOESN'T AUTOMATICALLY MAKE ANYONE VIRTUOUS.

only one form of capital, and that if you can cash it all in to "buy shares" in a more valuable form of capital, you should do it! Jesus reminds us that it's only money.

Jesus said, "It is more blessed to give than to receive,"[9] and in fact, studies support this notion. Michael Norton, an associate professor at Harvard Business School, conducted a study that indicates that when money is invested *in others* instead of ourselves, it actually increases our happiness.[10] It turns out money *can* buy happiness—you just need to invest it right (in others instead of ourselves).

The second way we get into trouble is by **devaluing financial capital entirely**, looking at it as somehow evil or tainted. Since overvaluation is a problem on one end of the spectrum, we figure that devaluing money entirely must be the virtue on the opposite side. Many people take pride in the fact that they "don't care about money," and have very little of it.

But not having money doesn't make anyone virtuous or happy, as anyone who has lived in poverty knows. Being poor doesn't automatically make anyone virtuous, just as having a lot of money doesn't make someone evil. A lack of financial capital is a lack, a limitation. Many people who take pride in having very little money are dependent on those who have some to spare.

It's important to acknowledge that there is nothing inherently wrong with having money, even with having a lot of it. Many of the patriarchs in the Old Testament (Abraham, Isaac, Joseph, etc.) were very wealthy people. Nowhere does the Bible say that money is evil.

· · · · · · · · ·

[9] Acts 20:35
[10] For more on the study, see Norton's TED Talk entitled "How to Buy Happiness," http://www.ted.com/talks/michael_norton_how_to_buy_happiness.html

The *love* of money is a massive problem, of course (which is the overvaluing problem). But we needn't throw out the baby (financial capital) with the bathwater (the love of money). Living hand-to-mouth isn't holier than being wealthy.

. . . .

A NOTE ABOUT PROSPERITY THEOLOGY

We want to say a word about so-called prosperity theology, which teaches that God wants his people to prosper financially. First, taken at face value, saying that God wants his people to prosper is often quite right. God certainly wants his children to have everything they need, just as we want the same for our own children. Jesus told us that if we know how to give good gifts to our children, why would we assume God isn't as good as we are? God *does* want his children to have enough, to prosper.

We see this throughout the Scriptures (which is the truth the prosperity gospel people are picking up on). God blessed Abraham, Isaac, and Jacob, and part of that blessing included financial wealth. In fact, Isaac became so wealthy and powerful that his neighbors asked him to move away, and then later asked him to move back because they realized they were enjoying the overflow of God's blessings to Isaac.[11] Financial blessing is not excluded from the ways God seeks to bless his children.

LIVING HAND-TO-MOUTH ISN'T HOLIER THAN BEING WEALTHY.

So what's the problem with prosperity theology? The problem is when it *equates financial capital with spiritual capital*, assuming that our financial abundance is an accurate way of measuring our spiritual abundance. It's easy to fall into this trap, because financial capital is the most measurable and concrete kind of capital

[11] You can find the account in Genesis 26:12-31. It's almost funny.

(because people have been measuring it longer than the others). Prosperity theologians tend to treat financial capital as the same thing as spiritual capital, and so they serve Money *as* God. This ultimately causes their theology as a whole to be unbalanced and unhelpful.

The fact is, there's a whole lot more to a well-lived life and prosperity than money. There are at least *five* capitals, and the other four are more valuable than financial capital. These other four capitals have a currency that allows us to measure their growth, but we're just not as familiar with those metrics, and so we tend not to think about or focus on those kinds of capital.

But that doesn't mean we can't! With a little thought and intentionality, we can begin to focus on the more important capitals and see whether we are growing in them. There's a lot more to life than getting more money, as we've already seen in our study. For example, Joseph (a son of Jacob) was sold into slavery by his own brothers. He ended up in Egypt as a slave in the household of a man named Potiphar. As a slave, he had *zero* financial capital, and yet in that situation, the Bible says, "The Lord was with Joseph so that he prospered."[12] Obviously, his prosperity wasn't financial. It's described in other terms. But it's still prosperity, because the Bible says it is!

Another example can be found in 3 John 2, where John prays that the recipient of the letter would prosper in "all respects," that he would be in good health, "just as your soul prospers." The writer is giving us a holistic view of prosperity that is a helpful corrective against the myopic focus of the so-called prosperity gospel. John is saying that *every area of your life should prosper*, not just one or two. He describes prosperity in terms of multiple kinds of capital and currency.

· · · · · · · ·

[12] Genesis 39:2

This way of looking at prosperity helps keep everything in proper orientation and guards us against the excesses of a narrow focus on only one area of capital apart from the others. Whenever we extrapolate a truth beyond its biblical context, we end up in trouble. A narrow focus on the humanity of Jesus becomes heresy because it's separated from the biblical context that also talks about the divinity of Jesus. Similarly, a narrow focus on financial capital (apart from the biblical context of the other capitals) yields the unhelpful "prosperity gospel," while a narrow focus on spiritual capital (apart from the biblical context of the other capitals) yields Gnosticism or something like it.[13]

Actually, we could say that the problem with prosperity theology is that it doesn't aim high enough. It's narrowly focused on measuring financial prosperity when it ought to be thinking about spiritual, relational, physical, and intellectual prosperity, too. It follows the way of the world in valuing financial capital above all else, instead of recognizing financial capital in its proper biblical place. We think financial capital is the ceiling when it's actually only the floor. As we'll see in a moment, keeping the capitals *in order* is really important.

The apostle Paul knew how to keep these things integrated, and he learned something important about financial capital. He said, "I have learned to be content whatever the circumstances. I know what it is to be in need, and I know what it is to have plenty. I have learned the secret of being content in any and every situation, whether well fed or hungry, whether living in plenty or in want." What was his secret? "I can do all this through him who gives me strength."[14]

Paul's life wasn't filled with constant financial abundance, and neither should we expect ours

• • • • • • • • •

[13] Gnosticism taught that we embrace the spiritual world by shunning the material world.
[14] Philippians 4:11-13

to be. Paul had seasons when he was in need, and he also had seasons when he had plenty. In *all* of those circumstances, Paul was able to function in his identity and calling, because of the strength that Jesus gave him. When finances were low, he knew he still had other kinds of capital that were worth far more than mere money. So whether he had plenty of money or very little money, he could still do everything he needed to do through the grace of God.

Financial capital, when put in its proper place, can be an important tool in bringing blessing to ourselves and others. But it's only one of the five capitals, and the least valuable one at that. The key is keeping it in its proper place and doing things the Jesus way, through him who gives us strength. After all, it's only money!

INTELLECTUAL CAPITAL

INTELLECTUAL CAPITAL IS HOW MUCH **CREATIVITY, IDEAS, AND KNOWLEDGE** WE HAVE TO INVEST. THE CURRENCY OF INTELLECTUAL CAPITAL IS **CONCEPTS AND IDEAS**, INFORMATION AND APPLICATION.

Next up on the hierarchy is **intellectual capital**. This refers to the knowledge we've acquired as well as our ability to bring ideas and creative solutions to the table. This is of higher value than financial capital, because you can't create ideas and inspire creativity simply by spending a lot of money. Intellectual capital comes from something deeper than what money can buy. You can throw all the money in the world at a problem, but it won't get solved until someone brings some intellectual capital to bear on the situation to come up with a creative and workable solution.

Jesus possessed an astonishing level of intellectual capital, which he used often in his mission. In the culture of his day, Jesus was recognized by the crowds, his disciples, and even his enemies as a rabbi, which means "teacher" or "master." A rabbi was a teacher

JESUS POSSESSED AN ASTONISHING LEVEL OF INTELLECTUAL CAPITAL, WHICH HE USED OFTEN IN HIS MISSION. of the Jewish law, someone who had studied very rigorously, someone who knew what he was talking about. In fact, after Jesus was resurrected, the first word out of the mouth of the first person to see Jesus alive was, "Rabboni!" (a form of rabbi).

Jesus wasn't just a holy person who prayed a lot—he was also a smart person who thought a lot. He had intellectual capital, and he used it to train his disciples, teach the crowds, and answer his detractors.

After a little talk he did on a hillside (traditionally called the Sermon on the Mount), the Bible says, "the crowds were amazed at his teaching, because he taught as one who had authority, and not as their teachers of the law."[15]

When the Pharisees (a religious sect within Judaism) tried to trap Jesus by asking him a tricky and politically loaded question about paying the imperial tax to Caesar, he answered in an astonishingly clever and prophetic way. Finding the coin used to pay the tax, Jesus asks them, "Whose image is this? And whose inscription?"

"Caesar's," they replied.

So Jesus answered them, "So give back to Caesar what is Caesar's, and to God what is God's."

The Bible simply says, "When they heard this, they were amazed. So they left him and went away."[16]

· · · · · · · · ·

[15] Matthew 7:28-29
[16] Matthew 22:15-22

That same day the Sadducees (another religious sect) tried to trap Jesus with an obtuse question about marriage laws. He answered them with such clarity and biblical insight that when the crowds heard it they were "astonished at his teaching."[17]

In addition to answering the Pharisees and amazing the crowds, Jesus used his intellectual capital mainly to train his disciples. He was constantly explaining his parables to the disciples, teaching them to understand the kingdom of God at a very deep level.

In short, Jesus was no slouch when it came to intelligence. He had boatloads of intellectual capital and used it to bless and serve the people around him.

PHYSICAL CAPITAL IS HOW MUCH **TIME AND ENERGY** WE HAVE
TO INVEST. THE CURRENCY OF PHYSICAL CAPITAL IS
HOURS AND HEALTH.

As we ascend our hierarchy of capital, **physical capital** is next. This refers to our ability to devote time and energy to people and projects. It comprises the time we make available as well as the capacity we have to use that time. Our overall health comes into play here, because it greatly affects our ability to invest our time and energy.

One key way we can invest in physical capital is simply honoring the limitations we have as humans. Getting proper rest and living in a rhythm of life that allows us to work hard *and* play hard is essential if we are going to steward our long-term physical capital. Jesus shows us how to do this. Obviously Jesus had a body, which was his "power pack"

• • • • • • • • •
[17] Matthew 22:23-33

JESUS CONSTANTLY STEWARDED HIS PHYSICAL CAPITAL AND TRAINED HIS DISCIPLES TO DO THE SAME.

of physical capital that allowed him to heal, preach, and train his disciples. He did not bypass the normal disciplines that need to accompany being a human being. He slept at night most of the time, walked from place to place, used language to communicate ideas, touched people as he healed them, and sat down and ate regular meals with others. He got tired when he did all those things, so he sometimes needed to take a nap! This is normal human stuff.

Paul encourages the Ephesians to invest their physical and intellectual capital wisely when he writes, "Be very careful, then, how you live—not as unwise but as wise, making the most of every opportunity, because the days are evil. Therefore do not be foolish, but understand what the Lord's will is."[18]

Jesus constantly stewarded his physical capital and trained his disciples to do the same. After Jesus sent his disciples out on their first short missionary journey during which they did the same things they saw him doing, things started to get quite busy. "Then, because so many people were coming and going that they did not even have a chance to eat, he said to them, 'Come with me by yourselves to a quiet place and get some rest.'"[19]

Jesus taught his disciples that there are seasons of bearing fruit and seasons of "abiding" when the fruit is pruned back and we spend a season *not* visibly bearing fruit.[20] Like a vine branch that has been pruned back, we simply abide in the vine for a season, receiving

• • • • • • • • •

[18] Ephesians 5:15-17
[19] Mark 6:31
[20] John 15:1-8

nourishment from the vine while nothing is really happening on the outside. Jesus taught his disciples that we need to embrace the pruning seasons or we won't bear fruit.

These instructions mirrored God's design in creation, where he rested on the seventh day of creation, creating a model for humanity to take one day off out of seven, where we set our work aside and rest. This might not seem like that big of a deal, but when God wanted to tell his people the top ten things to remember about what it means to be his people, taking a day off came in at number four! "Remember the Sabbath day by keeping it holy."[21]

Many business leaders today recognize this. Every month at least, a new article or podcast promotes the benefits of taking proper time off from work, or how productivity actually *increases* when employees stop working long hours. Just do an Internet search for "benefits of taking a day off," and you'll see dozens of articles. Whether you call it a mental health day or just plain-old vacation, the results are in—investing in our physical capital pays huge dividends in the long run.

Jesus, of course, knew this (brilliant economist that he was!). Physical capital is quite valuable, and worth stewarding well. Investing in our ability to spend time on people and projects shouldn't be taken for granted. It needs to be invested in intentionally.

As a side note, some people wonder if physical capital should be ranked higher than intellectual and financial capital. Think about it this way: If you're sick, you can't work (financial capital). Likewise, if you have a migraine, you can't deliver a lecture or read a book (intellectual capital). You can't solve a problem in a brainstorming meeting if you're

· · · · · · · · ·

[21] Exodus 20:8-11

---

in the hospital because of a heart attack. No amount of money or ideas can replace the value of being physically present, giving time and attention to people or projects. The health of our bodies, which translates into our ability to invest time and energy, is of significant value.

RELATIONAL CAPITAL

RELATIONAL CAPITAL IS HOW MUCH **RELATIONAL EQUITY**
WE HAVE TO INVEST. THE CURRENCY OF RELATIONAL CAPITAL IS
FAMILY AND FRIENDS.

Relational capital is next on the list. It refers to the quantity and quality of our relationships with others. Having family and friends is extremely valuable, and the amount of relational capital we have accrues to us in many ways, from our overall sense of well-being and happiness to more tangible ways. For example, if you lose your job and get kicked out of your apartment (to use an extreme example), you'd better have some friends and family you can stay with for a while. When you lose your ability to gain financial capital, you lean on the relational capital you've built up.

This is essentially what the rich man's manager was doing in Jesus' parable in Luke 16 that we discussed. He knew he was about to be fired (losing his financial capital), so he said, "I know what I'll do so that when I lose my job here, people will welcome me into their houses." He then used the financial capital still at his disposal to "buy friends" (grow his relational capital) so he would have a place to stay when he lost his job. It's fascinating that Jesus explicitly says to do this at the end of the parable: "Use worldly wealth to gain friends for yourselves." It's a wise investment!

The classic movie *It's A Wonderful Life* is all about the value of relational capital. James

Stewart plays George Bailey, a normal guy who sacrifices his dreams of traveling the world and decides instead to stay in his hometown of Bedford Falls, marry his sweetheart, start a family, and open up a building and loan company that functions as a bank to help people get loans to buy houses. He is a kind-hearted and compassionate man, allowing people to delay repayment of their loans when times are hard, refusing to foreclose on anyone who is attempting to pay back his loan.

When one of his partners misplaces a large cash deposit, the building and loan is in danger of going bankrupt, and George is at risk of going to jail for mismanagement of funds. He despairs and stumbles out to the bridge, contemplating suicide, believing his family and friends would have been better off without him. That's when an angel named Clarence visits and shows him what Bedford Falls would have been like if he'd never been born. George realizes that he has made a tremendous impact on the people around him in the ordinary things he has done his whole life. He realizes he has made many investments in relational capital for many years.

Thankful for this new realization of how truly rich he is, even though he is financially bankrupt, he returns to his wife and kids almost delirious with joy, shouting, "I'm going to jail!" In the final scene of the movie, the town finds out about his plight and the money he needs to deposit, and all of the people he's poured into over the years stop by to offer what they can in the way of financial assistance. With all of the friends who stop by, the total reaches the amount of the deposit that his partner lost. George Bailey stays out of jail and realizes what an incredibly rich community he has helped build.

This classic movie is essentially a story of investing in relational capital for a long time, and how it can be converted into financial capital in his hour of need. It's a story about relational capital being far more valuable than financial capital.

THE COVENANT RELATIONSHIP JESUS FORGED WITH HIS DISCIPLES FORMED THE BASIS OF THE KINGDOM BREAKTHROUGH HE WAS ABLE TO ACHIEVE THROUGH THEM.

Relational capital is more valuable than physical, intellectual, and financial capital because you really can't do anything of value in life without a relationship with someone where there is at least some level of mutual trust. In essence, you can't really *do* anything with your physical, intellectual, or financial capital unless you have at least a little relational capital.

In the Gospels, we see Jesus consistently invest in relational capital and train his disciples to do the same. Once he chose twelve of his disciples to be designated "apostles," he prioritized his time and investment in those twelve, developing deep relational capital with them as he trained them. We also see him repeatedly returning to the home of Mary, Martha, and Lazarus in Bethany, cultivating relational capital with them and using their home as a base of operations as well as a place of retreat.

Jesus was growing his relational capital by investing his physical capital in his covenant relationships. The covenant relationship Jesus forged with his disciples formed the basis of the kingdom breakthrough he was able to achieve through them.

Interestingly, it appears that investing relationally in this way was one of the ways Jesus paid his bills. At one point, Jesus is traveling from village to village with his twelve disciples, "and also some women who had been cured of evil spirits and diseases. These women were helping to support them out of their own means."[22] Jesus is investing relational capital and receiving financial capital.

· · · · · · · · ·

[22] Luke 8:2-3

SPIRITUAL CAPITAL

SPIRITUAL CAPITAL IS A WAY OF TALKING ABOUT THE DEPTH OF
OUR RELATIONSHIP WITH GOD AS A DISCIPLE OF JESUS, WHICH
RESULTS IN A KIND OF **SPIRITUAL EQUITY** THAT WE CAN
INVEST IN OTHERS. THE CURRENCY OF SPIRITUAL CAPITAL IS
WISDOM AND POWER THAT COME FROM HEARING WHAT GOD IS
SAYING AND RESPONDING WITH FAITH AND OBEDIENCE.

Jesus carried more spiritual capital than any other human being before or since. The
two things that people around him were constantly amazed at were his *teaching*, which
reflected a large store of wisdom that he shared, and his *miracles*, which reflected the great
amount of power that flowed through his life. When we grow in spiritual capital, we grow
in wisdom and power. **Wisdom is where knowledge and love kiss each other, and
power is simply operating in Christ's authority with his resources.**

According to Jesus, **spiritual capital** is the most valuable of all. It is more important than
relational capital, physical capital, intellectual capital, and financial capital. This is clear
from the entire ministry of Jesus. When Jesus talked about life in the kingdom of God and
how it was worth cashing everything else in for, he was talking about a life rich in spiritual
capital. When Jesus talked about eternal life, he wasn't talking just about long-lasting
life—he was talking about a life rich in spiritual capital that lasts forever. The kingdom of
God and eternal life are like code words to refer to a life filled with spiritual capital.

In fact, you could say that Jesus' whole mission was to help people prosper in spiritual
capital (and through spiritual capital, all the other capitals). His message was that through
relationship with him, anyone could become wealthy in spiritual capital. Isn't that an
interesting way to think about it? That was actually the gospel, or "good news," that Jesus
announced to people.

In the ancient world, they had a word for an official proclamation of good news. For example, if a new king had come to power, heralds would travel from place to place making the announcement of the good news that this new king was now ruling. The word they used for this good news was "gospel."

This is the word Jesus used to talk about his mission. "The time has come," he announced. "The kingdom of God has come near. Repent and believe the good news (gospel)!"[23] The good news that Jesus proclaimed was that life with God in his kingdom (which essentially means "under his rule") was now available to anyone who wanted it.

In business terms, one could say that a new market of incredible value was opening, and anyone had a chance to stake a claim in this new market. Jesus viewed life in God's kingdom as more valuable than anything else. Having spiritual capital is of the utmost value, and it's completely *available* to anyone who wants to get in on it. You don't need to be any particular race or gender, and you don't need to have a certain amount of money or status. The incredibly good news is that spiritual capital is astronomically *valuable* and radically *available*!

THE INCREDIBLY GOOD NEWS IS THAT SPIRITUAL CAPITAL IS ASTRONOMICALLY VALUABLE AND RADICALLY AVAILABLE!

(Incidentally, this got Jesus into a lot of trouble with certain folks who were quite interested in closing off the kingdom of God market to others, but that's another story for another time.)

So how do we enter the market of growing our spiritual capital? Jesus said we "repent and believe" the good news. These old-timey-sounding words essentially mean something very simple:

[23] Mark 1:14-15

WE LISTEN TO THE WORDS OF JESUS, AND WE PUT THEM INTO PRACTICE.

We listen to the words of Jesus, and we put them into practice.

Repent simply means to "change your mind." So we listen to what Jesus says, and we believe he is telling us the truth, and we say yes to him (and no to whatever we were thinking before). We agree with him about reality. This is what repentance is—listening to what Jesus says and surrendering to it.

Believe simply means to trust Jesus and to put that trust on display by *taking action*. Believing means that we trust Jesus enough to put his advice into practice. It's not saying we believe something exists—it's putting active trust in a person. For example, it's one thing for us to say that we believe airplane pilots exist, but it's another thing entirely for us to get on an airplane that's about to take off. One doesn't really require anything from us, while the other means we need to trust that pilot to fly me safely to my destination. Trust is displayed in action.

After one of his greatest sermons, Jesus told a parable that helped drive this point home. He said,

> *"Therefore everyone who hears these words of mine and puts them into practice is like a wise man who built his house on the rock. The rain came down, the streams rose, and the winds blew and beat against that house; yet it did not fall, because it had its foundation on the rock. But everyone who hears these words of mine and does not put them into practice is like a foolish man who built his house on sand. The rain came down, the streams rose, and the winds blew and beat against that house, and it fell with a great crash."* [24]

· · · · · · · · ·

[24] Matthew 7:24-27

The interesting thing is that both builders in the story heard the words of Jesus. Perhaps they agreed with the words or even felt inspired by them. The only difference was that one of the builders *put them into practice*, and this made all the difference.

Putting Jesus' words into practice makes us like a wise builder. Hearing Jesus' words but doing nothing about them makes us like a foolish builder. Putting Jesus' words into practice is how we grow our spiritual capital.

In practical terms then this is how we enter the market of spiritual capital. We listen to Jesus' words and put them into practice. As we walk through life, as we read Scripture, as we work and rest and play, we ask:

1. What is God saying to me?
2. What am I going to do about it?[25]

It's really that simple. The astonishing thing is that anyone can do it.

As we repent and believe, our spiritual capital grows, which means we gain more and more wisdom, and more and more power flows through our life, because **wisdom and power are the currency of spiritual capital**. They are what we have that grows when we cultivate a relationship of hearing and doing with God through Jesus. Spiritual capital is the fruit of our ongoing relationship with God, in which we develop an ever-deepening conversation of hearing his word to us and responding in surrender and obedience.

PUTTING JESUS' WORDS INTO PRACTICE IS HOW WE GROW OUR SPIRITUAL CAPITAL.

[25] We have developed a tool called the Learning Circle that helps people answer these questions. You can read about it in our book *Building a Discipling Culture*.

. . . .
Reflection Questions:

1. Out of the five forms of capital, which was the one that felt
    like a new idea to you? Why?

2. Have you ever thought about your relationships with family
    and friends as a form of capital that can grow or decline?

3. What are the implications of seeing our relationship with God
    as a form of capital that we can invest in?

CHAPTER 5 | **KEEPING THINGS IN ORDER**

We've learned that God wants to see us flourish not just in one area of capital, but in all five. A well-lived life means abundance in *all five* capitals.

If we're going to live well, we also need to pay close attention to **the value order of the five capitals**.

The five capitals are set up in a hierarchy that identifies their relative value, and it's very important to *keep things in that order, investing as though the most important things are actually most important.* For example, if we have an opportunity to invest some of our financial and physical capital to grow our spiritual capital (paying a spiritual director or coach, for example), this should be a no-brainer. We are investing a lower-value capital (financial) to grow a higher-value capital (spiritual).

Yet it's somewhat difficult to keep these things in proper perspective. Most of us don't automatically make financial investments to grow our spiritual capital, because we probably overvalue financial capital. Why is this?

One problem is that we tend to build our investment strategies on "quick returns" rather

**THERE ARE QUITE
A FEW COMPETING
VALUE SYSTEMS
OUT THERE.**

than patiently waiting for more valuable investments to mature over time. Financial capital gives us the quickest return, and so we tend to focus our investment strategies there. All the capitals above financial take longer to grow, but they are also more valuable and last longer. Spiritual capital, the most valuable capital, lasts *forever*. But it also takes the longest to grow.

Another reason it's difficult for us to keep our capitals in their proper place is that the institutions and cultures of our day (just as the ones in Jesus' day) tend to put the five capitals in a different order, and relentlessly train us to think similarly. There are quite a few *competing value systems* out there.

. . . .
CAPITAL IN THE BUSINESS WORLD

For example, let's think about the *business world*. In it, financial capital is valued most highly. The profit motive specifically points to *financial* profit. Everything else is leveraged to grow financial capital. Getting more money is seen as the point of business. So the business world might list the five capitals in the following order of value:

1. **FINANCIAL**

2. **INTELLECTUAL**

3. **RELATIONAL**

4. **PHYSICAL**

5. **SPIRITUAL**

After the ultimate goal of making money (financial capital), ideas and creativity are the next highest capital (intellectual capital), because they can be leveraged for more money. After that comes relational capital, since business happens only where relationships are strong. Physical capital is near the bottom, because it's generally acceptable to sacrifice your health to work more hours, and last on the list is spiritual capital, because it's rarely even considered to have any value at all as a capital in the business world.[26]

If we've been influenced by the business world, no wonder it's difficult to keep our concerns about financial capital in check. We have been trained to think it is the most important capital, when it is in fact the *least* important.

When we think financial capital is most important, we are willing to sacrifice all kinds of other capital to get it. Working late at the office might get us a great bonus at the end of the year, but in doing so we sacrifice relational capital with our children, who wish we were home to tuck them in at night. We also sacrifice our physical capital, as we work so much our health begins to fail. We sacrifice spiritual capital because we don't attend to our relationship with Jesus (spiritual capital) at all for some time. Eventually, life stops working properly, because we've made a foolish investment, sacrificing capital that was in fact more valuable (spiritual, relational, physical) to grow capital that was less valuable (financial).

Here's another way this plays out: Moving halfway across the country to take a great job opportunity is regarded as wise and sensible, but moving halfway across the country to join a great community is regarded as foolish and a little weird. It's so automatic for us to prioritize financial capital that we are willing to throw away a *lot* of relational capital to get

• • • • • • • • •

[26] Interestingly, there are signs that this is changing. August Turak's book *The Business Secrets of the Trappist Monks*, for example, outlines the business benefits of a focus on spiritual capital.

a little more financial capital, but it seems like a strange decision to sacrifice some financial capital in order to grow our relational capital.

This is actually the story of everyone who has joined the 3DM team over the years. Nobody has ever moved here because of a job offer. All of them moved here to join a family on mission, trusting that the financial stuff would work out. And it has! Once people got here, something eventually needed to be done, and jobs would get created. But the point was that they didn't move here for a job; they moved to join a family, and often a job came as a byproduct. As the family grows, the family business grows, so it just makes sense.

So if we've got our capitals in order, we ought to prioritize the *who* question before the *what* question. Who is the family we are called to be on mission with? Let's invest our capital to be part of that family and trust that the relational capital we build will eventually translate into financial capital that we can live on. The fact that this paragraph sounds strange to our ears is a testament to how backwards we have gotten this.

. . . .
CAPITAL IN THE ACADEMIC WORLD

How about another example? Let's think about the *academic world*. There, the capital of highest value is probably *intellectual*. Accumulating and passing on knowledge are seen as the highest good in the academic environment. We're just guessing here, of course, but perhaps the order goes something like this:

1. **INTELLECTUAL**

2. **FINANCIAL**

3. **RELATIONAL**

4. **PHYSICAL**

5. **SPIRITUAL**

The life you get when you invest in this order is a different kind of life from the one you get when you invest in the business world order. Spending vast amounts of money to get a Ph.D. is seen as a worthy investment, because intellectual capital is valued more highly than financial capital. But spiritual capital is again at the bottom, as Jesus is not taken seriously in the academic world as someone who has *knowledge* about life.

Sigmund Freud is an example of the sad result of investing everything for intellectual capital and valuing it above the other capitals (thus out of its proper place in the hierarchy). On September 22, 1939, Freud pulled a copy of Honoré de Balzac's *The Magic Skin* off his library shelf and read the entire book in one sitting.

Balzac wrote *The Magic Skin* in 1831, telling the story of Raphael, a young doctor who craves recognition and wealth that seemed consistently to elude him. After he gambles away his last coin, he sets off to throw himself into the Seine River to commit suicide. But on the way, he stumbles upon a small shop with exotic items from all over the world. In that shop, he finds a "magic skin" from the Orient. The shopkeeper tells him that whoever wears it will get anything he desires, but with every act of self-willfulness, the skin will shrink and slowly squeeze out his life. The shopkeeper tells him it's free, but advises that he not take it. But the broke and ambitious doctor takes the magic skin and puts it on. He immediately desires a huge party with dancing, drink, and food, and instantly he gets it.

At first, he indulges whatever wishes he feels deep within, but the more he gets, the less satisfied he is. He desires more and more, but his skin gets tighter and tighter, squeezing the life out of him. He eventually falls in love with a woman named Pauline, but his deep desire for her shrinks his skin even more. In the climax of the story, Pauline visits Raphael in his room and expresses her love for him. But when she learns the truth about the magic skin and her role in Raphael's demise, she is horrified. Raphael cannot control his desire for her, and so she rushes into an adjoining room to escape him and thus save his life. He pounds on the door and declares his love and his desire to die in her arms. She, meanwhile, is trying to kill herself to free him from his desire. Raphael succeeds in breaking down the door and rushes to Pauline, only to die—squeezed, suffocated, and strangled—in her arms. It's quite an intense story!

After reading the novel, Freud called in his physician, Dr. Schur, and reminded the doctor of a promise he had made earlier to help him commit suicide: "You promised me then not to forsake me when my time comes. Now it's nothing but torture and makes no sense anymore." After a heavy dose of morphine, injected twice twelve hours apart, Sigmund Freud died at 3:00 A.M. Freud, one of the most successful, renowned, influential men of the twentieth century, pursued intellectual capital above all and in the end lost everything in despair.[27]

· · · · · · · · ·

[27] This telling of Freud's death is taken largely from Larry Crabb's article "The Sure Route to Madness," found in the first issue of *Conversations: A Forum for Authentic Transformation*. http://conversationsjournal.com/wp-content/uploads/2012/10/Conversations_Journal_Issue_1_1.pdf

CAPITAL IN THE CHURCH

Another example: *church*. How do most churches value the five capitals? How does yours? It'd be great to say that spiritual capital is the highest, but do we actually behave as though it is? What gets discussed at board meetings? What are our measurements of success? What is the thing that assumed to be the highest good? The thing we leverage all our capital for? Isn't it usually to get more people to come to church and for the giving to increase?

Perhaps the order looks something like that in many churches:

1. **PHYSICAL** (attendance)

2. **FINANCIAL** (tithes and offerings)

3. **RELATIONAL**

4. **SPIRITUAL**

5. **INTELLECTUAL**

Of course every tradition is a bit different. For example, the more historic denominations (like the one Mike belongs to!) are often very influenced by the academic world, valuing intellectual capital much more highly than spiritual capital. This ends up affecting the way we do theological education, the way we place value on leaders, what we are willing to invest money in, and more.

We bring this up so we will recognize that even our church cultures can train us to value the five capitals in a way that puts them in the wrong order. *Any* wrong order always leads to foolish investments and a life that *just doesn't work.*

. . . .

CAPITAL IN YOUR FAMILY

One more example: How is capital valued in your family? What about your family of origin? What kinds of things are invested in consistently? Do you have an "academic achievement" culture that values intellectual capital above everything else? Would you rather sacrifice a good night's sleep to get an "A" on that test, or go to bed on time and settle for a "B"?

How about a family culture that values the "athletic opportunity" above all else, placing physical capital at the top of the list? For example, how much family time is sacrificed so that the kids can participate in sports? It's not wrong to play team sports, of course, just like it isn't wrong to get an "A" on a test, but it's worth asking the question of which capital is actually at the top of your list.

WE NEED TO VALUE THESE THINGS LIKE JESUS DID IF WE'RE GOING TO INVEST WISELY AND DEVELOP AND NURTURE THE LIFE WE'VE BEEN GIVEN.

Perhaps the family culture values Mom's or Dad's career above everything else. Advancement and promotion are the "highest good" to be sought, and other capitals are invested to make sure that the financial capital grows.

The point of asking all these questions is to point out that the institutions and cultures around us are actively training us to value things in a certain way, but we need to value these things like Jesus did if we're going to invest wisely and develop and nurture the life we've been given. We need to learn to value and invest the five capitals the way Jesus did, because he was the most brilliant economist and businessman who ever lived, and he leveraged all of his capital on our behalf.

. . . .
Reflection Questions:

1. Think about the way you invest your capital, and the things you leverage capital to get. If an objective observer looked at the way you spend your time and was asked to put the five forms of capital in value order for your life, what would that order be?

2. What would it look like for you to rearrange the way you value the five forms of capital so they line up with the way Jesus says they matter?

CHAPTER 6 | **INVESTING FOR A RETURN**

So how do we grow our capital, especially the most important ones? It's actually pretty simple, and you may have already thought of it. **The way we grow our capital in one area is by investing what we have of the other four.** Let's get practical about how this works.

GROWING YOUR FINANCIAL CAPITAL

As we think about growing our financial capital, it's important to remind ourselves again that this only works when financial capital is kept in its value order, serving the other capitals, especially spiritual capital. From that place of orientation, then, we want to remember that our financial capital belongs to God, and we are in charge of it. That's why we often use the word *stewardship* to talk about the way we relate to our financial capital. Being a steward means we're in charge of someone else's stuff.

Understanding that it all belongs to God, and we are called to be good steward's of God's stuff, we can operate in **generosity instead of stinginess** (this is the transformation Ebenezer Scrooge goes through in Charles Dickens' *A Christmas Carol*).

From this place of *generosity*, then, let's think about what might need to happen to grow our **financial capital**. People do this all the time—start with nothing and eventually grow their financial capital. Every time people start a business, they are investing other forms of capital to grow financial capital. Perhaps they invest intellectual capital by bringing a brilliant business idea, a new product, or an invention to the table. The iPhone and Facebook are great examples of intellectual capital being invested to grow financial capital.

But the idea isn't enough. We'll need to put in lots of hours working, investing physical capital. We'll need to leverage our relational networks to get the word out about our new venture, as well as cultivate relationships with potential customers, investing relational capital. When you think about it, even a loan from a bank is a form of relational capital that you are leveraging to grow your financial capital. Last, of course, any wisdom (spiritual capital) we have acquired will be invested in the way we run our new business. Perhaps it makes us sacrificial and kind as a leader instead of self-serving and cruel, all helping us grow our financial capital.

Here's an example. One current 3DM team member needed to grow their financial capital in order to make it possible for them to move their family to Pawleys Island, South Carolina (where 3DM is headquartered) and be part of the community here. There was no money for a position at 3DM, but this person felt called to join us.

So he invested his intellectual capital by using his counseling background to create a coaching business. He invested his physical capital by spending more time and energy in the coaching business, getting the word out and gathering new clients. He invested his

THE POINT OF GROWING OUR CAPITAL IS NEVER JUST SO WE CAN HAVE MORE CAPITAL; IT'S ALWAYS SO THAT WE HAVE MORE TO SHARE.

relational capital by asking his current friends and family to tell others about his coaching business to see if they knew anyone who would be interested in it. He invested his spiritual capital by bringing his wisdom and insight to his coaching business, speaking wisdom from God into people's lives as opposed to just good advice.

The end result was that his financial capital grew to the point that he was making his living with the coaching business, which enabled he and his family to move to Pawleys Island and be part of the *oikos* here.

It's also worth noting that growing his financial capital wasn't the point in and of itself. The financial capital was necessary to enable him to move to Pawleys Island, which was how he was going to grow his family's and his spiritual and relational capital. The point of growing our capital is never just so we can have more capital; it's always so that we have more to share, which is actually an investment that helps us grow the most valuable capitals.

GROWING YOUR INTELLECTUAL CAPITAL

As we've said, financial capital, while necessary, is the least important of the five. What would it look like to grow the other capitals? Let's look at how we can invest the other four capitals to grow our **intellectual capital**.

How can we grow in our ability to both think creatively, coming up with great ideas, and

WE CAN'T GROW OUR QUANTITY OF TIME, BUT WE CAN GROW THE QUALITY WITH WHICH WE USE OUR TIME.

communicate those ideas effectively to others? Perhaps we spend money to take a night class (investing financial and physical capital). Perhaps we call our friends and family to see if they have ideas or information that we could use (investing relational capital). Perhaps we pray and ask God for creativity, a new idea (investing spiritual capital).

The same team member who grew his financial capital to move to Pawleys Island recently completed advanced training in a variety of counseling tools. Essentially, what he is doing is *investing* financial and physical capital (money and time) to grow his intellectual capital.

Maybe you have lots of great content but need to invest in the ability to present it creatively. You could ask a creative friend to help you (investing relational capital to grow your intellectual capital). Maybe you've got loads of creativity but need to invest in getting some better ideas, so you take some classes to deepen your knowledge in a certain field. These ideas can get you started in how to grow intellectual capital.

GROWING YOUR PHYSICAL CAPITAL

Let's think about what it would look like to grow our **physical capital**. Although we might think it would be nice, we can't actually get any more time during the day. Everyone has the exact same amount of time available in a day. So we can't grow the *amount* of time we have, but we can grow our capacity to *use* our time well. We can't grow our *quantity* of time, but we can grow the *quality* with which we use our time.

The way we spend our time can be categorized as either *rest* or *work*. In fact, this is the way God set it up in the beginning, modeling and commanding a rhythm of rest and work that results in a well-lived and productive life. The command to take a day off every seven made it into the top ten commandments, in fact. It's pretty important to God for us to steward and grow our physical capital, honoring our need for seasons of both rest and work on a daily, weekly, and seasonal basis.[28]

One way to grow our physical capital is simply to take a day off once a week! Taking a day off is a way of investing financial capital to grow physical capital, since we are sacrificing a day of making money in order to rest. Set aside your urge to produce or fix and simply focus on resting, recreating, and enjoying life one day per week. Do it with your family, and you'll be growing your physical and relational capital.

Another way to grow our physical capital is to get healthier. Better health allows us to be better stewards of our time, because we have more energy for the tasks of the day and more mental clarity for problem-solving, and we don't get sick as much. Healthy people just get more done.

Since the currency of physical capital is time and energy, you might also consider investing in time-management skills. Many people find that, after taking a course or reading a book on managing their tasks and time better, they are more productive with their time at work, leaving more room for truly resting.

To grow your physical capital you might want to get a gym membership (investing

• • • • • • • • •

[28] For more on living in rhythm, see the chapter on the Semi-Circle in our book *Building a Discipling Culture*.

financial capital). You might want to read a few new books on eating better (investing intellectual capital). You might want to ask a friend to join you at the gym for some accountability (investing relational capital), and you might also make it a matter of prayer and study, looking at what Scripture says about the healthy rhythm of work and rest (investing spiritual capital).

GROWING YOUR RELATIONAL CAPITAL

How would you grow your **relational capital**? Jesus encourages us to "use worldly wealth to make friends," so it's not a bad idea to set some money aside to spend taking people out or having them over for dinner once a week (investing financial capital). Investing intellectual capital could look like helping people with things you know how to do and sharing your expertise with others, by working on their cars or helping them with their computers. Of course spending time with people (investing physical capital) is an indispensable part of any relationship, so if you want to grow your relational capital you'll need to plan to spend lots of time with people. You'll also want to invest your spiritual capital by praying for those with whom you want to grow in relational capital, and perhaps asking God to give you a word of encouragement for them.

RELATIONAL CAPITAL HAS TO DO WITH BUILDING A SENSE OF BOTH PLAY AND PURPOSE WITH THOSE IN RELATIONSHIP WITH YOU.

Relational capital has to do with building a sense of both play and purpose with those in relationship with you. *Play* is all about having fun with people, enjoying one another's company, laughing together, throwing parties together. *Purpose* is all about a community being called to selflessly serve a higher cause, with everyone pulling in the same direction. Cultivating *play* and *purpose* is important for growing relational capital as a family on mission.

When my wife and I (Ben) joined the 3DM team we wanted to grow our relational capital with the other members of the team, so we created a discipline of inviting one other family over once a week (investing financial and physical capital). We went out of our way to assist the other members of the team in our areas of knowledge and expertise (investing intellectual capital), and we often ended up sharing biblical wisdom and encouragement with others on the team (investing spiritual capital).

Another way to grow your relational capital is learning how to recognize people of peace. This phrase comes from Luke 10 where Jesus sends out his disciples to the places he is about to go, telling them to look for a "person of peace," in the villages they were being sent to. A person of peace is someone who likes you, welcomes you, and serves you in some way. This is an indication that God is at work in their life, and their openness to you means God is inviting you to be part of what he's doing![29]

Like all investment, growing your relational capital requires a discipline that produces a repeatable process that allows you to predictably and regularly invest in growing your capital.

GROWING YOUR SPIRITUAL CAPITAL

Finally, how do you grow your **spiritual capital**? Since it is the most valuable capital, this is an important question. This is something we should constantly be seeking to do, and

. . . .

[29] For more on people of peace, see the chapter on the Octagon in our book *Building a Discipling Culture*.

the good news is that it's actually something we can *always* be investing in. As with the other capitals, you grow your spiritual capital by investing what you have in the other four capitals.

The currency of spiritual capital is *wisdom and power*, exercised in the context of love, and the way we get it is simply by hearing God's word to us and responding in faith and obedience. **Hearing and doing** are the key disciplines we embrace if we want to grow in wisdom and power (our spiritual capital).

People who hear but don't do become "inspiration junkies." They love the experience of worship or prayer, but since they never really put anything into practice in their lives, they simply run from event to event, their lives remaining unfruitful. The Bible calls this "foolishness."

People who do but don't hear can fall into the trap of becoming "vapid activists." They love the rush they get from serving or organizing a mission trip, but because they don't take the time to listen to the leading of the Holy Spirit, all their frenetic activity bears very little fruit. The Bible calls this operating in "the flesh," meaning our normal human abilities apart from God's power.

We must be committed to hearing and doing to grow our spiritual capital. For example, you might take time off work to travel and meet with someone who could help you grow your spiritual capital, or buy books that will assist you in developing your spiritual capital (investing financial capital). You might offer your skills and knowledge to an organization that could help you grow your spiritual capital (investing intellectual capital). Remember, as you invest, you need to actually *put something into practice* as a result of these endeavors if you are to gain spiritual capital.

Perhaps you offer your time to serve someone who can help you grow your spiritual capital (investing physical capital). This is actually the very thing the disciples did with Jesus. The standard method of training in the time of Jesus was that a disciple would serve and support a rabbi who had spiritual capital, so that they could grow their spiritual capital. The disciples were investing their financial and physical capital to enable Jesus to invest his spiritual capital in them.

There are all kinds of other ways to invest to see spiritual capital grown. Perhaps you spend more time in prayer and Bible study for a season (investing physical capital). You can ask friends and family for their wisdom in situations and circumstances (investing relational capital). You get the picture.

As our capital grows in one area, we can then turn around and invest it to grow our capital in another area. For example, at 3DM we've found that as we've invested spiritual capital in others through Coaching and Learning Communities, very often we become good friends with them, and we develop long-term partnerships that bear good fruit for years to come. Our relational capital grew as a byproduct of investing our spiritual capital. There are countless other examples that remind us that growing in the five capitals takes time and intention.

Reflection Questions:

1. Think about the way you invest your capital, and the things you leverage capital to get. If an objective observer looked at the way you spend your time and was asked to put the five forms of capital in value order for your life, what would that order be?

2. What would it look like for you to rearrange the way you value the five forms of capital so they line up with the way Jesus says they matter?

CHAPTER 7 | **PRACTICAL STORIES OF INVESTMENT AND GROWTH**

Sometimes it's helpful to see a few concrete examples of how people have invested their capital and grown it. So in this chapter, we'll share stories of how some people have invested, grown, and shared the five capitals.

One family that recently joined the 3DM team moved quite a long distance to be here. One of their children was wrestling with the move a bit, asking why they had left the place they'd lived for fifteen years. The parents answered in terms of the five capitals:

> We are investing the lowest three capitals to grow the top two. We are investing financial capital (it cost a lot of money to move here), intellectual capital (bringing our expertise and creativity to benefit 3DM), and physical capital (we are giving our time and energy to the goals of 3DM). But as we do this, we are seeing our relational capital grow (new relationships with great people all over the world), and most importantly we are seeing our spiritual capital grow (being involved in this family on mission is helping us grow in wisdom and power and making us more fruitful).
>
> Even though you guys are still kids, you have a great chance to grow your spiritual

WHEN WE LOOK AT IT THIS WAY, WE AREN'T REALLY SACRIFICING, BUT TAKING ADVANTAGE OF A FANTASTIC INVESTMENT OPPORTUNITY.

and relational capital here. You can take advantage of the environment here to grow spiritually, and you have a chance to develop relationships with leaders all over the world. Who knows how that will pay off in the future?

When we look at it this way, we aren't really sacrificing, but taking advantage of a fantastic investment opportunity. We get to grow our capital in the two most important areas!

Here's another story of a woman who wanted to grow her spiritual capital:

I had been a Christian for 27 years, and had a relationship with Jesus, but I met a group of people who seemed to have something more . . . an intimacy with Jesus I didn't have (what I later learned to call spiritual capital, the most important kind). At the time I didn't have that language, though, so I just intuitively began to invest the capitals I did have to get the one I didn't have.

I invested my financial and physical capital (my money and time) to begin a coaching relationship with one of these people. I attended seminars and learning immersions. I took classes offered at church. I invested my intellectual capital (and again physical and financial) as I studied the Word of God and books on discipleship and relational intimacy with God. I drew on the relational capital I did have (though honestly that was also suffering) to bring my husband and children into this journey.

In the end, the blessing was that my spiritual capital grew. I experienced a life-changing breakthrough in the area of intimacy with Jesus, and began to grow in a naturally supernatural lifestyle. I feel more blessed than ever!

Dave and Kim Rhodes, along with another partner, founded a ministry to young adults called Wayfarer, which eventually merged with 3DM (and now functions as 3DM's student arm). Dave and Kim now function as the U.S. Team Leaders of 3DM.

Their story of starting Wayfarer is a fantastic example of the way it sometimes *seems* like financial capital is the most important because we don't think we can do what we're called to do without it. Money "makes the world go 'round," as they say. But if we keep the five capitals in the order Jesus taught we find that money becomes much less central and limiting because we are investing the four other capitals in a way that creates opportunities where money would have us believe there are only obstacles. The Rhodes' story is a great example of this.

> *It all started at Palm Beach Atlantic University. We were a bunch of guys who were doing life together, seeking God together, and we were seeing God show up in remarkable ways. Though we didn't have language for it at the time, we had essentially started a Missional Community, and the fruit of it was really sweet. It was a bunch of people living as a family, doing life together, seeing people come to Jesus and join us. It was awesome. When it was time to graduate, we asked the question, "Why does this have to stop? Who says this has to stop?" Again, although we didn't have language for it at the time, we were experiencing an abundance of relational capital and questioning why people simply drop all the relational capital they accumulate in college because it's the normal thing to do.*

> *In the meantime, we were beginning to expand our little family on mission—we met a ministry partner and began to lead summer youth camps together. Again, we had*

developed what was basically a Missional Community, an oikos—we traveled together, did life and ministry together. We built a friendship and eventually decided to go to seminary together (preserving relational capital instead of choosing to do these things individualistically, which is the normal way to do it). We moved to Birmingham, Alabama, for seminary, and eventually five or six of the other families we'd been doing life with came and joined us in Birmingham. We spent three and a half years there as an extended family on mission. We lived in the same apartment complex, doing life and mission together.

We came to the point of graduating, and another decision was upon us. What now? Again, the normal expectation is that everyone says their goodbyes and you go your separate ways, throwing away the relational capital. We decided to do something different. There were some opportunities locally, but we felt called to start something.

So we decided to start something. We didn't have any seed money, besides $2,000 out of our own pockets. We took stock of where we had other kinds of capital we could build on, and for a number of reasons we felt like the Greenville/Spartanburg, South Carolina, area was the place to start. We both had relational connections there (more relational capital), and it felt like God's grace was going before us.

So we moved there (before long, so did a few of the other families we'd been doing life with). We started Wayfarer in our partner's parents' basement (again, following the relational capital) and didn't take a salary for nine months. We paid the bills because both of our wives got jobs with another local company where we had relational connections. It allowed them to use their skills, but they got the jobs in the first place because of the relational capital we had with the owners.

**"WE DON'T HAVE
A JOB TO GIVE
YOU—WE HAVE AN
OPPORTUNITY TO
PUT IN FRONT OF
YOU."**

By now we had leveraged a lot of relational capital to get this thing started, and now that we were moving, it was time to leverage our intellectual capital to grow the business. Our intellectual capital consisted mainly of an ability to write and speak. We actually had a heart to start a ministry for local twenty-somethings, but we knew if we simply started there, we'd have to shut the whole thing down because twenty-somethings didn't have any financial capital, which is what we needed to pay the bills at the time. So we used our intellectual capital to create a business that developed curriculum and did communication at camps and other events. This eventually provided us with enough financial capital to enable us to do the local ministry among twenty-somethings that we wanted to do.

As the business grew, we needed more staff. But again, we didn't have any extra financial capital lying around, so we couldn't exactly hire people in the normal way. So we turned again to our relational capital when we'd talk with people about coming to join us. "We have an opportunity here," we'd tell people, "but no income. The opportunity isn't primarily about financial capital, it's about relational capital, and the testimony of our lives is that if you come and join us here as a family on mission, we as a family will make sure you get fed. We don't have a job to give you—we have an opportunity to put in front of you." The only way that makes any sense to people is if they can trust the relational capital to make the financial capital work.

We hired the next four or five people that way. They first moved to simply join the family, and in the process there was eventually enough financial capital to give them an official job. In the process, we grew our business from a budget of maybe $20,000 a year (85 percent of which came from ministry gifts and 15 percent from our self-sustaining efforts) to a budget of almost $750,000 a year (85 percent self-sustaining, 15 percent *ministry gifts). And none of that came with any seed money. It was relational seed that we leveraged for an opportunity to leverage our intellectual capital that eventually resulted in enough financial capital to make ends meet and do the local ministry we felt called to do, investing spiritual capital in twenty-somethings.*

Of course there was lots of spiritual and physical capital invested along the way. As in all startup businesses, we all worked lots of hours, we prayed a lot, and we constantly needed to rely on God going before us with his grace.

Here's another story from a woman who used the five capitals as a way to be more intentional about how she and her family spent their time on vacation:

One of the things my husband and I realized was that after we took a vacation we tended to feel slightly disappointed. We didn't feel like we had gotten everything out of it that we wanted to. Our huddle leader told us about the five capitals and suggested that for our next vacation we think about how to intentionally invest in growing the top four capitals (spiritual, relational, physical, and intellectual) during our vacation. We don't grow financial capital during vacation (by definition, we spend it, which is actually investing it to grow other kinds of capital), but we were learning to be more intentional about investing our financial capital and our time on vacation to grow the top four capitals.

So we thought through each one:

- *Spiritual: We committed to spending more time than usual every day in prayer, reading Scripture, etc.*

- *Relational: We chose specific people we wanted to connect with for supper, planned fun and engaging activities to do with our kids, made space for conversations with old friends, etc.*

- *Physical: We planned how much we were going to do our exercise routine, going for walks in the evening, getting enough sleep, getting massages, etc.*

- *Intellectual: We chose a few books to read through during our vacation that would broaden our minds and stretch us a bit intellectually.*

The first time we did this, we felt an amazing difference at the end of our vacation. We actually felt like the significant things had happened during our vacation, because we had invested in the top four capitals. Our times of rest used to feel scattered and purposeless, like we were just taking a break from working because we were tired. We were simply crashing from our striving. But now our times of rest feel like a vital part of a rhythm of life that results in fruitfulness and joy, part of an integrated life where we are always investing to grow our capital, so we have more to share.

One final story, about Sally and me (Mike). Often people wonder how we ended up starting 3DM in Pawleys Island, South Carolina. It's not exactly the most strategic place to set up the headquarters of an international organization. Most people have no idea where it even is! You can probably guess this by now, but the reason we ended up here has to do with return on investment in the five capitals.

Sally and I had been coming to Pawleys Island for eleven years before we moved there. A local pastor from our denomination had invited us to come and speak, so we'd come every year and speak a bit, bring pastors on retreat here, hold conferences and meetings, and

WE WERE SIMPLY INVESTING BECAUSE WE TRUSTED THAT GOOD INVESTMENTS GROW.

then take a bit of vacation at the beach with our family, which we (of course) loved.

As we went there year after year, we were investing our spiritual, relational, physical, and intellectual capital over and over. And quite frankly, I didn't know what (if anything) we were achieving. We were simply investing because we trusted that good investments grow. But we weren't really sure when, if ever, we'd see any kind of return.

When we needed to find a place to land and start 3DM, Pawleys Island ended up on the shortlist because of all the capital we had banked here. It seemed like a place of peace to us. People here welcomed us, liked us, listened to us, served us—all the marks of a Person of Peace.[30] We decided to go, since there were people here who seemed open to us and liked us.

Sure enough, when we arrived, people came out of the woodwork to give us a return on our investment. One significant person in the community who owns one of the nice houses on the beach found us and said, "You don't know this, but nine years ago you prayed for me, and God healed me of a terrible, embarrassing skin condition." That triggered a vague memory—at the end of one of my talks, I had a funny feeling that God wanted to heal people with an odd skin condition. I didn't even know what it was, but apparently God healed this person of it, and now she was in front of me telling me about it. So now, when

• • • • • • • • •

[30] For more on People of Peace and how they work in evangelism and mission, see the chapter on the Octagon in our book *Building a Discipling Culture*.

we have visitors come, they often stay at her beach house. That's the kind of return on investment that happens when we take the capital we have and invest it in others.

Here's a biblical example of investment. Acts 6 tells a story about investment and capital in the economy of the early church. The number of disciples was increasing, and a very normal thing happened—conflict. The Hellenistic Jews complained against the Hebraic Jews because they felt their widows were being overlooked in the distribution of food. (It's remarkable to think about how sophisticated a system of food distribution they must have had for this to even become an issue!)

The twelve apostles gathered to try to decide what to do. Verse 2 tells of their decision:

> *"It would not be right for us to neglect the ministry of the word of God in order to wait on tables. Brothers and sisters, choose seven men from among you who are known to be full of the Spirit and wisdom. We will turn this responsibility over to them and will give our attention to prayer and the ministry of the word."*

"This proposal pleased the whole group," the text says, and that's what they did. I've heard some commentators suspect that this wasn't actually the right decision on behalf of the apostles, that somehow they were trying to get out of the menial task of waiting on tables and making sure everyone got their fair share of food.

But if we look at it through the lens of the five capitals, we see that they weren't trying to avoid serving. They were simply recognizing that the best way for them to serve was not by waiting on tables, but by attending to prayer and the ministry of the word. They recognized that they were investing so much physical capital in the food distribution that they weren't able to invest their spiritual capital in the community. Waiting on tables is

**YOUNG MEN COME
IN AND SAY, "I'D
REALLY LIKE TO
FIND A WIFE."
AND I'LL SAY, "SO
WHAT'S YOUR
STRATEGY?"**

important, but for the early church community to grow as disciples of Jesus, they needed the apostles to attend to the more important matters of prayer and ministry of the word.

There were lots of godly people who could wait on tables, but the apostles were the only ones in the community who had spent three years with Jesus. Physical capital is valuable and necessary, but spiritual capital is *more* valuable, and the apostles had an abundance of spiritual capital to invest in the community. Freeing them up to do it was a great investment decision for the whole community.

Hopefully you can see from these examples how utterly practical this stuff is. We use investment in the five capitals as an analytical tool in all kinds of situations. For example, because we're ordained ministers, people often talk to us about pastoral issues, like finding a spouse. Young men come in and say, "I'd really like to find a wife." And we'll say, "So what's your strategy?"

> *"Well, I pray about it a lot."*

> *"That's good. Anything else?"*

> *"What do you mean?"*

> *"Well, you're investing your spiritual capital, which is great, but are you investing anything else in this project of finding a wife?"*

> *"I still don't know what you're talking about."*

"Well, you're talking about the most important relationship of your life. You'd better be investing more in it than a few prayers here and there. For example, how much money did you spend on your last date with this girl you've been seeing?"

"We just ate leftovers and watched a video."

"That's probably not going to cut it. You need to invest more financial capital than that, surely."

"I never really thought about it that way."

"And how about physical capital? You might want to get in shape a bit."

"That doesn't seem very spiritual."

"Ah, but it is! How do you expect to grow your relational capital in such a massive way unless you invest more of your current capital in the other areas?"

We could literally go on and on with examples of investment and growth in the five capitals. It's one of the most practical ways to get a handle on what it looks like to live what Jesus called an *abundant life*.

And the beautiful thing about living an abundant life is that it doesn't only bless us, but everyone around us as well. We get a return on our investment, and so do others! The more we have, the more we have available to invest in others. This is actually the whole point. When our capital grows, we aren't the only ones who benefit—everyone around us benefits as well, because we share our capital with others (which is actually *investing* it, after all). Because we invest in others, we see a return on that investment in another area, which gives us more capital to invest into others.

This is what happened in the accounts of the early church in Acts. They leveraged all of their capital on behalf of one another, which caused all of their capital to grow. So they had more to invest in others, so it continued to grow, so they had more to invest, and on and on it went in a virtuous cycle (the opposite of a vicious cycle).

Imagine a whole community doing this together—investing its capital in each other, seeing it grow and grow. It becomes a very beautiful family on mission, because when our capital grows, it doesn't just benefit us as individuals. The whole community is lifted up and given an opportunity to grow its capital together.

. . . .
Reflection Questions:

1. **Can you think of any stories in your past in which you invested in any of the five capitals without realizing it?**

2. **How do the stories strike you? Does it seem like a strange thing to value relational and spiritual capital so highly? Why or why not?**

CHAPTER 8 | **HOW YOU CAN START INVESTING TODAY**

We're sure you're getting the picture by now. But before we end this book, one more question—**how can you start to invest and grow your capital today?** Let us suggest a simple exercise that will help get the ball rolling. You may want to do this exercise together with those in your household or business, but it can work for an individual, too.

First, take stock of your current situation. Write down each of the five capitals in order, and put **one of three symbols** after each capital.

- An **UP ARROW** next to the capitals that are currently **growing**
- A **DOWN ARROW** next to the capitals that are currently **diminishing**
- A **SIDEWAYS ARROW** next to capitals that are currently **staying the same**

Here's an example:

1. SPIRITUAL CAPITAL

2. RELATIONAL CAPITAL

3. PHYSICAL CAPITAL

4. INTELLECTUAL CAPITAL

5. FINANCIAL CAPITAL

Obviously, the ideal situation is that all your capital is growing, but seeing areas where you are static or diminishing gives you pertinent information you need for your future investment strategy.

Now that you know the direction your capitals are moving, **take stock of how much relative *equity* you have in each area of capital**. You'll remember that each capital has its own currency, but for the sake of this exercise, pretend you cashed in all the different kinds of currency for gold bars.

After you calculated the various exchange rates, you ended up with seventeen gold bars, which represents the current capital God has given you.

So you have seventeen gold bars. **Distribute those seventeen gold bars across the five capitals** in a way that accurately reflects how much equity you think you have in each area of capital.

Here's an example:

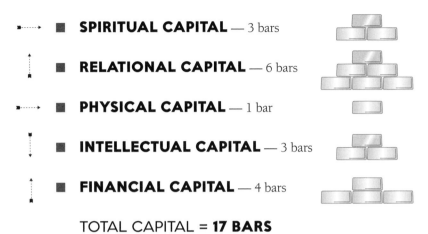

SPIRITUAL CAPITAL — 3 bars

RELATIONAL CAPITAL — 6 bars

PHYSICAL CAPITAL — 1 bar

INTELLECTUAL CAPITAL — 3 bars

FINANCIAL CAPITAL — 4 bars

TOTAL CAPITAL = **17 BARS**

The reality, of course, is that we don't all have the same amount of capital. Some will have more, some less, just like in Jesus' parable. But this exercise will begin to help you discern how your current capital is distributed and if it's going up or down, which will help you develop an investment strategy.

Now that you've assessed your capital's distribution and direction, let's recall Jesus' parable in Matthew 25. A master was going on a journey, and he entrusted his wealth to his servants in various amounts. When the master returned, he found that two servants had doubled their investment while one servant did nothing with it, literally burying it in the ground to hide it.

Part of the point of the parable is that we are called to be like the servants who doubled their investment. If God has entrusted us with some of his capital, we ought to be seeking to invest that capital and see a return. So let's assume we did what the two servants did: We invested our capital and doubled our investment. **This means you now have seventeen *more* gold bars, for a total of thirty-four**.

Add those new gold bars to your current totals in a way that demonstrates **how you would like to *grow* your current capital**, keeping in mind your current equity level and whether each kind of capital is growing, diminishing, or staying the same.

In the example above, the physical capital is quite low and diminishing. We will definitely want a strategy to grow our physical capital. Maybe we decide that we'd like to grow it significantly, from one bar to six bars. That takes up five of our additional seventeen gold bars, leaving us with twelve to distribute in the other capitals.

Here's an example fleshing out the rest of this growth plan:

- ■ **SPIRITUAL CAPITAL** — From 3 bars to 8 bars
- ■ **RELATIONAL CAPITAL** — From 6 bars to 8 bars
- ■ **PHYSICAL CAPITAL** — From 1 bar to 6 bars
- ■ **INTELLECTUAL CAPITAL** — From 3 bars to 5 bars
- ■ **FINANCIAL CAPITAL** —From 4 bars to 7 bars

   TOTAL = 34 BARS (ADDING 17)

Now you know the areas where you want to grow your capital. The final part of this exercise is to devise a plan for *how* you will actually grow in each of those areas of capital.

Remember that to grow one capital, we need to find ways to invest the other four capitals. And remember that investment is simply a discipline that turns into a repeatable process. Another word for that is rhythm or routine. **What rhythms and routines can you use to invest your current capital and achieve the growth you're looking for in all five capitals?**

For example, if you want to grow your spiritual capital from three bars to eight bars, you'll need to invest financial, intellectual, physical, and relational capital to do so.

Get specific with this question. **What practical, measurable, concrete investment routines and rhythms can you put in place that will grow your capital?** If it's not on the calendar, it's probably not an actual practice.

Take some time to reflect and discuss this with others in your household as you create an intentional strategic plan for growing your capital in the next season. Put it on the calendar, and grow your capital.

INVESTING IN OTHERS / MAKING DISCIPLES

As we close this book, it's important to remember *why* we are seeking to invest and grow our capital in all five areas. This isn't some kind of private enrichment program—it's how we **participate with God in what he's doing in the world**. The true wealth we are growing is not just for ourselves; it's to be shared. There's a word for this: *commonwealth*, which essentially means the wealth that is held in common with others in the community. We need to reclaim this word.

Commonwealth is a great picture of *oikonomics*. It describes wealth that is

1.   In all five capitals
2.   Valued in the correct order
3.   Shared with our *oikos*

A family on mission that is growing in its common capital can't help but be an attractive community that shows the world something about the future toward which God is pulling us.

Jesus shows us that God is doing is moving us steadily toward his ultimate goal, which is described in the last book of the Bible, Revelation:

**THIS ISN'T SOME KIND
OF PRIVATE ENRICHMENT
PROGRAM—IT'S HOW WE
PARTICIPATE WITH GOD
IN WHAT HE'S DOING IN
THE WORLD.**

Look! God's dwelling place is now among the people, and he will dwell with them. They will be his people, and God himself will be with them and be their God. He will wipe every tear from their eyes. There will be no more death or mourning or crying or pain, for the old order of things has passed away.[31]

This is a description of the **maximum abundance** of every capital.

- **SPIRITUAL** — God dwelling among his people, and his people knowing him completely and cooperating with him fully.

- **RELATIONAL** — No more war or conflict between people; instead, perfect relational harmony and peace.

- **PHYSICAL** — No more death or sickness; instead, perfect health for our bodies and environment.

- **INTELLECTUAL** — Creativity and ideas abound. (You didn't think heaven would be boring, did you?)

- **FINANCIAL** — No more poverty or lack of any kind, but abundance of everything needed for a full life.

This is God's goal, for everyone to share in an abundance of spiritual capital, which causes

· · · · · · · · · ·

[31] Revelation 21:3-4

flourishing in all the other areas of capital. God's heart is for the **holistic flourishing** of his creation in all five areas of capital.

When you ask people what they think heaven is like, nobody ever says, "It's a poverty-stricken place where everyone is sick and living alone with no friends." Nor is that the picture the Bible paints! The biblical vision of heaven is of a place where all five capitals are maxed out in abundance! If that is our eternal inheritance, and we have an opportunity to grow into it now, why wouldn't we do it?

The truth is that Jesus didn't teach us to just sit around and wait for it—he taught us to actively pursue it *now*. He taught us to pray for God's kingdom to *come* (here), for his will to be done *on earth as it is in heaven* (now). The flourishing of heaven is meant to touch our lives and our neighborhoods *today!*

The way that God achieves this goal is, remarkably, through his people. God has invested in us, and like the master in the parable of the talents, he is looking for a return on that investment, desiring that it will bear fruit and grow and be invested in others for the flourishing of all humanity. The return God gets on his investment is that more and more people come to know him and begin to function as humans were meant to function, prospering in all of the five capitals and investing in others so they too can prosper in the five capitals. God's heart from the very beginning has been the blessing of all people, the flourishing of humanity.

THE BIBLICAL VISION OF HEAVEN IS OF A PLACE WHERE ALL FIVE CAPITALS ARE MAXED OUT IN ABUNDANCE!

How do we learn to do this? **We become disciples of Jesus**, the best economist and investment strategist the world has ever known. He is the one who guides us into living out our purpose. His call isn't for us to just grow our own capital. Your personal prosperity is not the point. The point is growing what you have *so you can invest it into others* and see a return, as you participate in the mission of God.

As disciples of Jesus, we learn to live like Jesus and invest like Jesus. How do we make disciples? **We invest everything we have in all five capitals into others.** Making disciples means investing *everything we have*—all five capitals—into those we are discipling. It's a call to lay it all down, to invest everything, on behalf of those we are investing in, trusting that when they win, we win, and when people win, God wins. **We grow our capital to invest our capital for others, which causes our capital to continue to grow.**

Learning to invest in the five capitals is a win/win/win scenario. There's no downside! And it's 100 percent guaranteed by God to produce a life worth living.

Sell everything and buy the field. The treasure is worth far more than you could possibly imagine.